CHRIST IN ISAIAH

CHRIST
in
ISAIAH

F. B. Meyer

OLIPHANTS

OLIPHANTS
BLUNDELL HOUSE
GOODWOOD ROAD
LONDON S.E.14

First Lakeland Edition 1970

SBN 551 00047 3

PRINTED IN GREAT BRITAIN BY
WILLMER BROTHERS LTD, BIRKENHEAD
AND BOUND BY C. TINLING AND CO. LTD, PRESCOT

Contents

Preface

The Exodus from Egypt is one of the most conspicuous landmarks of the past; not only because of its historical value, but because it inaugurated a religious movement which is the most important factor in our modern world.

The Exodus from Babylon has never succeeded in arousing equal interest, largely because it was more gradual and uneventful. Yet it was a marvellous episode, and bore upon its face the evident interposition of Jehovah on behalf on his people. Its results, which culminated in the advent of the Servant of the Lord, were in the highest degree momentous.

The story of this Exodus is anticipated in chapters 40 to 55 of the Book of Isaiah, which form the subject of this volume. But the story of the Exodus itself is subsidiary and introductory to another theme, which soon absorbs our attention. Before us pass, in vivid outlines, the scenes by which our redemption was secured. The humiliation and suffering, sorrow and anguish of soul, substitution and death, exaltation and satisfaction of the Saviour are portrayed, with the minuteness and accuracy of a contemporary; and there is hardly a sentence from which we cannot begin and preach Jesus, as Philip did to the Ethiopian eunuch.

F. B. MEYER

1

"COMFORT YE, COMFORT YE"

"Ask God to give thee skill
In comfort's art ;
That thou mayst consecrated be
And set apart
Into a life of sympathy.
For heavy is the weight of ill
In every heart ;
And comforters are needed much
Of Christlike touch."

. A. E. Hamilton

(Isaiah 40:1)

Think it not strange, child of God, concerning the fiery trial that tries thee, as though some strange thing had happened. Rejoice! for it is a sure sign that thou art on the right track. If in an unknown country, I am informed that I must pass through a valley where the sun is hidden, or over a stony bit of road, to reach my abiding place—when I come to it, each moment of shadow or jolt of the carriage tells me that I am on the right road. So when a child of God passes through affliction he is not surprised.

In the case of the chosen people, who for nearly seventy years had been strangers in a strange land, and had drunk the cup of bitterness to its dregs, there was thus added weight to their sorrow—the conviction of their captivity being the result of their own impenitence and transgression. This is the bitterest of all—to know that suffering need not have been ; that it has resulted from indiscretion and inconsistency ; that it is the harvest of one's own sowing ; that the vulture which feeds on the vitals is a nestling of one's own rearing. Ah me! this is pain! There is an inevitable Nemesis in life. The laws of the heart and home, of the soul and human life, cannot be violated with impunity. Sin may be forgiven ; the fire of penalty

9

may be changed into the fire of trial: the love of God may seem nearer and dearer than ever and yet there is the awful pressure of pain; the trembling heart; the failing of eyes and pining of soul; the harp on the willows; the refusal of the lip to sing the Lord's song.

We cannot wonder at the troubles that afflict us. *Look up.* Thou art to be like the Son of God, who Himself passed through the discipline of pain, as the participator with the children of flesh and blood. If He needed to come to earth to learn obedience by the things that He suffered, surely thou canst not escape. Couldst thou be quite like Him, unless thou art perfected by suffering? Thou must endure the file of the lapidary; the heat of the crucible; the bruising of the flail—not to win thy heaven, but to destroy thy unheavenliness. The spirits gathered on the frontiers of the heavenly world, to encourage thee in thy journey thither, tell thee that the brilliance of their reward has been in the measure of the vehemence of their sorrows, giving scope and opportunity for the heroism of their faith.

Look down. Thinkest thou that the prince of hell was pleased when thou didst forsake him for thy new master, Christ? Verily not! At the moment of thy conversion, thy name was put on the proscribed list; and all the powers of darkness pledged themselves to obstruct thy way. Remember how Satan hated Job; does he not hate thee? He would vent on thee the hatred he has to thy Lord, if he might. There is, at least, that one case on record of hell being permitted to test a saint, within a defined limit.

Look around. Thou art still in the world that crucified thy Lord, and would do the same again, if He were to return to it. It cannot love thee. It will call thee Beelzebub. It will cast thee out of its synagogue. It will count it a religious act to slay thee. In the world thou shalt have tribulations, though in the midst of them thou mayest be of good cheer.

When the soul is in the period of its exile and bitter pain, it should do three things: Look out for comfort; store it up; and pass it on.

(1) LOOK OUT FOR COMFORT.—It will come *certainly*. Wherever the nettle grows, beside it grows the dock-leaf;

10

and wherever there is severe trial, there is, somewhere at hand, a sufficient store of comfort, though our eyes, like Hagar's, are often holden that we cannot see it. But it is as sure as the faithfulness of God. "I never had," says Bunyon, writing of his twelve years' imprisonment, "in all my life, so great an insight into the Word of God as now; insomuch that I have often said, Were it lawful, I could pray for greater trouble, for the greater comforts' sake." God cannot forget his child. He cannot leave us to suffer, unsuccoured and alone. He *runs* to meet the prodigal; but He rides on a cherub, and He *flies* on the wings of the wind to the sinking disciple.

It will come *proportionately*. Thy Father holds a pair of scales. This on the right is called As, and is for thine afflictions; this on the left is called So, and is for thy comforts. And the beam is always kept level. The more thy trial, the more thy comfort. *As* the sufferings of Christ abound in us, *so* our consolation also aboundeth through Christ.

It will come *Divinely*. It is well, when meeting a friend at the terminus, to know by what route to expect him, lest he arrive on one platform, whilst we await him on another. It is equally important to know in what quarter to look for comfort. Shall we look to the hills, the stable and lofty things of earth? No; in vain is salvation looked for from the multitude of the mountains. Shall we look to man? No; for he cannot reach low enough into the heart. Shall we look to angels? No; among the many ministries that God entrusts to them, He seldom sends them to comfort; perhaps they are too strong, or they have never suffered. To bind up a broken heart requires a delicacy of touch which Gabriel has not. God reserves to Himself the prerogative of comfort. It is a Divine art. The choice name of the Son and the Spirit is Paraclete (the Consoler or Comforter). Thine is the God of all comfort. It is when Israel is in the extremity of her anguish, that the Divine Voice sounds from heaven in strains of music, "Comfort ye, comfort ye, My people, saith your God. Speak ye comfortably to Jerusalem." "I am He that comforteth you." "As one whom his mother comforteth, will I comfort you."

It will come *mediately*. What the prophet was as the spokesman of Jehovah, uttering to the people in human tones the inspirations that came to him from God, so to

11

us is the great Prophet, whose shoe-latchet the noblest of the prophetic band was not worthy to unloose; and our comfort is the sweeter because it reaches us through Him. In these words we hear the Father calling to the Son, and saying, "Comfort ye, comfort ye, my people." "Our comfort aboundeth *through Christ.*"

It will come *variously.* Sometimes by the coming of a beloved Titus; a bouquet; a bunch of grapes; a letter; a message; a card. Sometimes by a promise; the laying of an ice-cold cloth on our fevered brows; sometimes by God coming near. See in this chapter the variety of considerations by which God would comfort the despondent soul. That the term of sorrow is nearly accomplished; that herald voices announce the levelling of difficulties, and the approach of dawn; that the covenant stands sure; that the God of stars and worlds is the tender Shepherd, who will not overdrive his flock; that man at his strongest is but the flower of grass, whilst God's Word is like the great mountains. There are many strings in the dulcimer of consolation.

In sore sorrow it is not what a friend says, but what he is, that helps us. *He* comforts best who says least, but simply draws near, takes the sufferer's hand, and sits silent in his sympathy. This is God's method. "Thou drewest near in the day that I called upon Thee: Thou saidst, Fear not!"

(2) STORE UP COMFORT.—This was the prophet's mission. He had to receive before he could impart. He had to be schooled himself before he could teach others.

The world is full of comfortless hearts. Orphan children are crying in the night. Rachels are weeping for their children. Strong men are crushed in the wine-press, because their blood is the life of the world. Our God pities them. He cannot stay the progress of these awful years, until the mystery of iniquity is finished. Still He pities, and would assuage the anguish of the world through thee. But ere thou art sufficient for this lofty ministry, thou must be trained. And thy training is costly in the extreme; for to render it perfect, thou must pass through the same afflictions as are wringing countless hearts of tears and blood. Thus thy own life becomes the hospital ward where thou art taught the Divine art of comfort. Thou art wounded, that in the binding up of thy wounds

12

by the Great Physician thou mayest learn how to render first aid to the wounded everywhere. Thy limbs are broken, that in the setting of them thou mayest have a personal acquaintance with the anatomy and surgery of the heart.

Dost thou wonder why thou art passing through some special time of sorrow? Wait till ten years are passed. I warrant thee, that in that time thou wilt find some, perhaps ten, afflicted as thou art. Thou wilt tell them some day how thou hast suffered and hast been comforted; then as the tale is unfolded, and the anodynes applied which once thy God had wrapped around thee, in the eager look and glistening eye, and the gleam of hope that shall chase the shadow of despair across the soul, thou shalt know why thou wast afflicted, and bless God for the discipline that stored thy life with such a fund of experience and helpfulness.

Store up a careful memory of the way in which God comforts thee. Watch narrowly how He does it. Keep a diary, if thou wilt, and note down all the procedure of his skill. Ponder the length of each splint, the folds of each bandage, the effect of each opiate, cordial, or drug. This will bring a twofold blessing. It will divert thy thoughts from thy miseries to the outnumbering mercies; and it will take away that sense of useless and aimless existence which is often the sufferer's weariest trial.

(3) PASS ON THE COMFORT YOU RECEIVE.—At a railway-station a kind-hearted man found a schoolboy crying, because he had not quite enough money to pay his fare home. Suddenly, he remembered how, years before, *he* had been in the same plight, but had been helped by an unknown friend, who enjoined him some day to pass the kindness on. Now he saw that the anticipated moment had arrived. He took the weeping boy aside, told him the story, paid his fare, and asked him, in his turn, to pass the kindness on. And as the train moved from the station, the lad cried cheerily, "I will pass it on, sir." So that act of wonderful love is being passed on through the world, nor will it stay till its ripples have circled the globe and met again.

"Go, and do thou likewise." "Speak comfortably to Jerusalem, and cry unto her." God comforteth thee, that thou mightest comfort those who are in any trouble. Thou

13

canst not miss them: they are not scarce. Thine own sad past will make thee quick to detect them, where others might miss them. If thou findest them not, seek them; the wounded hart goes alone to die. Sorrow shuns society. Get from the Man of Sorrows directions where the sorrowing hide. He knows their haunts, from which they have cried to Him. He has been there before thee. And when thou comest where they are, do for them as the Good Samaritan did for thee, when He bound up thy wounds, pouring in oil and wine. "Comfort ye, comfort ye, My people, saith your God."

2

VOICES THAT SPEAK TO THE HEART

"The world were but a blank, a hollow sound,
If He that spake it were not speaking still;
If all the light, and all the shade around
Were aught but issues of Almighty will.

"Sweet girl, believe that every bird that sings,
And every flower that stars the elastic sod,
And every thought that happy summer brings
To thy pure spirit, is a word of God."

H. Coleridge

(Isaiah 40: 2)

When the heart is sad, and the years bring no relief, be sure to turn from the fret of circumstance, the confused murmur of human life, the many voices that speak from the crowds around; and listen with ear intent, until the soul distinguishes those other deeper voices that penetrate the barrier of sense from the land of the unseen, where God is, and life is at the full. There may be no shape or form, no speaker that can be recognised, no angel-messenger with radiant glory and wing of noiseless strength; but there will be voices, not one or two only, but sometimes, as in this marvellous paragraph, *four* at

14

least. Each the voice of God, but each with a different accent, a different tone.

The anonymity of the voices is unimportant. The multiplication table is anonymous; but it is not less true. Some of the sweetest of the Psalms, and the Epistle to the Hebrews are anonymous; but they carry their credentials on their face, everywhere in their fabric is the hall-mark of inspiration. That these voices speak out of the void, borne down the wind from eternity, whilst the heralds themselves are veiled in twilight which is slowly opening to dawn, makes nothing against their credibility and comfort. A strain is sweet, though we know not the composer; a picture is noble, though we know not the artist; a book is true and helpful, though no name stands on the title-page. The heart of man, made in the image of God, recognises instinctively the voices that speak from God; as a child, far from home in the blackest night, would recognise instantly any of the voices that it had been wont to hear from its cradle-days.

This is one characteristic of the voices that reach us from God: *They speak home to the heart* (R.V., marg.). The phrase in the Hebrew is the ordinary expression for wooing, and describes the attitude of the suppliant lover endeavouring to woo a maiden's heart. Love can detect love. The heart knows its true affinity. Many voices may speak to it, but it turns from them all; it heeds them not; till one day the true prince sounds on the horn the blast for which all was waiting—the spell is broken, and the sleeping maiden awakes to welcome her true lover. So thy heart will recognise its Immortal Lover by this token. "I was asleep, but my heart waked; it is the voice of my Beloved that knocketh."

(1) THE VOICE OF FORGIVENESS.—The first need of the soul is forgiveness. It cannot endure suffering; and if that suffering, like that of the Jewish exile, has been caused by its own follies and sins, it will meekly bow beneath it, saying with Eli, under similar circumstances, "It is the Lord; let Him do what seemeth good to Him." But the sense of being unforgiven! God's clouded face! The dark shadow on the heart! Neither sun nor star shining for many days! The oppressive weight of unforgiven sin! The question whether God's mercy may not be clean gone for ever, and that He will be favourable no more!

15

This bitterness of heart for sin is the first symptom of returning life. It does not justify, but it prepares the soul eagerly to seek and tenaciously to hold God's method of righteousness. And before God can enter upon his great work of salvation, before He can clear away the debris and restore the ruined temple, before He can reproduce his image, it is needful to assure the penitent and believing soul that its time of service is accomplished, that its iniquity is pardoned, and that it hath received at the Lord's hand double for all its sins.

In dealing with the question of sin and its results, let us always distinguish between its penal and natural consequences. The distinction comes out clearly in the case of drunkenness or criminal violence. Society steps in and inflicts the penalties of the fine, the prison, or the lash ; but in addition to these, there is the aching head, the trembling hand, the shattered nervous system. So in respect to sin. Its violation of the holy law of God ; its affront to the majesty of Divine government ; its personal injury to the Lawgiver—could only be atoned for by the death of the Second Man, the Lord from heaven. He bore our sins in His own body on the tree—He put away sin by the sacrifice of Himself. He was made sin, therefore our trespasses cannot be imputed to us ; and God in Him has reconciled the world unto Himself.

But the natural consequences remain. David was forgiven, but the sword never left his house. The drunkard, the dissolute, the passionate, may be pardoned, and yet have to reap as they sowed. The consequences of forgiven sin may be greatly sanctified ; the Marah waters cured by the tree of the cross—yet they must be patiently and inevitably endured. It was thus that Jerusalem was suffering, when those dulcet notes reached her. She was loved with an everlasting love. Though the literal city was in ruins, and her sons in exile, yet to God they were Jerusalem still—"Speak ye comfortably to *Jerusalem.*" But, nevertheless, the backsliding and rebellious people were doomed to serve their appointed time and captivity, and suffer the natural and inevitable results of apostasy. Hence the double comfort of this announcement ; not only that all iniquity was pardoned, but that warfare was accomplished, and that she had suffered double enough of natural punishment to serve the Divine purpose of sanctification.

16

Thou too hast been suffering bitterly. Those early indiscretions and errors of thy life have brought a terrible revenue of pain. Thou hast passed many days over a path paved by burning cinders, and thy feet are blistered. But God will not always be threshing thee. The sword shall not devour for ever. The billows of the sea shall pursue thee to their limit, but not beyond. Thy time of hard service as a conscript (lit. rendering) is accomplished, thine iniquity pardoned, thou hast received double for all thy sins. It has appeared to come from thy foes; but it has been meted out by the Lord's hand, and He says, It is enough.

(2) THE VOICE OF DELIVERANCE.—Between Babylon and Palestine lay a great desert of more than thirty days' journey. But the natural difficulties that seemed to make the idea of return chimerical, were small compared with those that rose from other circumstances. The captives were held by as proud a monarchy as that which refused to let their fathers go from the brick-kilns of Egypt. Mountains arose in ranges between them and freedom, and valleys interposed their yawning gulfs. But when God arises to deliver his people who cry day and night unto Him, mountains swing back, as did the iron gate before Peter; valleys lift their hollows into level plains; crooked things become straight; and rough places smooth.

When Eastern monarchs travel through their dominions, they are preceded by couriers, who require the towns through which they pass to repair the roads and highways. This is the purport of the herald voice, which rings out on the startled and trembling silence, "Prepare ye in the wilderness the way of the Lord, make straight in the desert a highway for our God"; and which foretells the levelling of obstacles, as a woman's hand may smooth creases out of linen, or the steam roller level the sand.

If thou hadst ears to hear, thou too shouldst hear it. Thou art sitting solitary and desolate; the Lord's song has long been hushed on thy tongue; the hand of the oppressor is heavy; and it seems useless to expect other deliverance than that of death. Thou hast, like Job, courted and fondled the idea of dying. "Now should I have lien down and been quiet; I should have slept; then had I been at rest." But God has some better thing awaiting thee in the near future, when his glory is revealed. Dawn is at hand, and with dawn deliverance.

It seems impossible. The tangle is so great, the obstacles so many, the hold of captivity so tenacious. There are, doubtless, smiling Italian landscapes; but the Alps stand as an impassable barrier, with inaccessible crags, and walls of ice, and yawning crevasses. Things are too crooked ever to be straightened in this world; too rough to admit of further progress, which is as impossible as of sledges over hummocks of ice. But wait only upon God; let thine expectation be from Him. He will come with a strong arm; and as He leads thee forth—as the angel led Peter—to thine amazement insuperable obstacles shall disappear: Red Seas and Jordans shall yield pathways; mountains shall fill valleys; ropes shall be as tow in flame; and netted snares shall be like cobwebs, which a touch destroys.

(3) THE VOICES OF DECAY AND IMMORTAL STRENGTH.—As man's soul is still, and becomes able to distinguish the voices that speak around him in that eternal world to which he, not less than the unseen speakers, belongs, it hears first and oftenest the laments of the angels over the transience of human life and glory. In a stillness, in which the taking of the breath is hushed, the soul listens to their conversation as they speak together. "Cry," says one watcher to another. "What shall I cry?" is the instant inquiry. "There is," continues the first, "but one sentiment suggested by the aspect of the world of men. All flesh is grass, and all its beauty like the wild flowers of the meadow-lands, blasted by the breath of the east wind, or lying in swathes beneath the reaper's scythe."

The words meet with a deep response in the heart of each thoughtful man. "Man cometh forth as a flower, and is cut down." "As for man, his days are as grass; as the flower of the field, so he flourisheth." We have all seen it. Our goodly sons, our sweet, fair girls, our little babes, have faded beneath our gaze, and lie among the grass of ordinary folk. Jerusalem had long been in exile; one by one her heroes and defenders, her statesmen and prophets, had died in captivity. Her sons were now of a smaller type. Nehemiahs in the place of Isaiahs; Ezras instead of Jeremiahs; Zerubbabels for Hezekiahs. Where was the Moses to lead this second Exodus; the

18

Joshua to settle them in their land; the Solomon to build their temple? There seemed no reply, save that given by the sigh of the wind from the great Lone-land, and the edge of Death's sharp reaping-hook. Thus the deliverers and champions of earlier days have passed away. Who now shall succour?

But listen further to the voices of the heavenly watchers. The failure of man shall not frustrate the Divine purpose. Lover and friend may stand aloof, or be powerless to help; the strong arm may be powerless to fulfil its olden promises; the prop of the family may have fallen; the bread-winner may be on his bed, unable to do aught to maintain wife and children: but God will do as He has said. He is independent of men and means. He can make ravens bring food. "The grass withereth, the flower fadeth; but the Word of the Lord shall stand for ever."

It is good to hear this angelic testimony to the permanence of the Word of God. Of course we could not doubt it. By it were the heavens made, and all the host of them; and by it the wheel of natural revolution is ever kept in motion; and yet since our all depends on it, since it is the basis of our hope in the Gospel, we may be forgiven for hailing gladly the confirmation of heavenly testimony, that the Word of God shall stand for ever.

(4) VOICES TO HERALD THE SHEPHERD-KING.—The Old Version and the margin of the R.V. are perhaps preferable to the R.V. Zion, the grey fortress of Jerusalem, is bidden to climb the highest mountain within reach, and to lift up her voice in fearless strength, announcing to the cities of Judah lying around in ruins that God was on his way to restore them. "Say unto the cities, Behold your God! Behold the Lord God will come."

All eyes are turned to behold the entrance on the scene of the Lord God, especially as it has been announced that he will come as a mighty one. But, lo! a Shepherd conducts His flock with leisurely steps across the desert sands, gathering the lambs with His arm, and carrying them in His bosom, and gently leading those that give suck. It is as when, in after centuries, the beloved apostle was taught to expect the Lion of the tribe of Judah, and, lo! in the midst of the throne stood a Lamb as it had been slain.

Do not be afraid of God. He has a shepherd's heart

and skill. He will not over-drive. When He puts forth his own sheep, He will certainly go before them, and they shall follow Him. He will suit his pace to theirs. Words can never tell his tender considerateness. If the tract lies over difficult and stony roads, it is because there is no other way of reaching the rich meadow-lands beyond. When strength fails, He will carry thee. When heavy demands are made, He will be gentleness itself. He is the Good Shepherd, who knows his sheep, as the Father knows Him.

These are the voices that speak to us from the Unseen. Happy is he who makes a daily parenthesis of silence in his heart, that he may hear them speak. It was a good habit of a devout servant of God to sit before the Lord for an unbroken period at the end of each day, that he might hear what God the Lord might speak. Ours be the cry of Samuel, "Speak, Lord, for thy servant heareth."

3

"WHY SAYEST THOU?"

"Go, count the sands that form the earth,
The drops that make the mighty sea;
Go, count the stars of heavenly birth,
And tell me what their numbers be;
And thou shalt know love's mystery."

T. C. Upham

(Isaiah 40: 12-31)

It is well in times when feeling is strong to say little, lest we speak unadvisedly with our lips, murmuring at our lot, or complaining against God, as though He had forgotten to be gracious, and had shut up his tender mercies in anger. Speech often aggravates sorrow. We say more than we mean; we drown in the torrent of our words the still small voice of the Holy Ghost whispering comfort; we speak as though we had not known or heard. It is wise, therefore, not to pass grief into words. Better let

20

the troubled sea within rock itself to rest. "Why sayest thou, O Jacob, and speakest, O Israel?"

Was it a true thing these exiles said? They suggested that they had worn out the Divine patience; that their way was no longer open to his view; and that their judgment had ceased to be his care. They were ready to admit that He had been the God of their fathers; but He had now withdrawn from his covenant relationship, and would be favourable no more. That, they said, was the reason why they were allowed to languish year after year on the plains of Babylon. They spoke as though they had never known nor heard some of the most rudimentary facts about the nature and ways of God. "Hast thou not known? Hast thou not heard?"

In our dark hours we should revert to considerations which have been familiar to us from childhood, but have of late ceased to exert a definite impression. It is remarkable what new meaning sorrow discovers in truths familiar as household words. It looks for the hundredth time into their abyss, and suddenly sees angels sitting. Let us recount some of these familiar facts; and perchance, as thy troubled soul turns from men and things, from what depresses and what threatens, to the everlasting God, the Lord, the Creator, thou wilt dare to believe that He has neither forgotten nor forsaken thee; that He delights still in thy way, which is leading through the tangled thicket into the sunlight; that He is weighing thy case with infinite solicitude.

Nature has always been the resort of the suffering. Elijah to Horeb; Christ to Olivet. And in these glowing paragraphs, which touch the high-water mark of sacred eloquence, we are led forth to stand in the curtained tent of Jehovah, to listen to the beat of the surf, and watch the march of the stars.

A passage from the journal of a sad and lonely thinker, with singular beauty of language, tells the effect of Nature upon him. He is speaking of the month of April; and after alluding to the moist freshness of the grass, the fragrance of the flowers, the transparent shadows of the hills, the breath of the spring, he says: "There have been so many weeks and months when I thought myself an old man, but I have given myself up to the influence of my surroundings. I have felt the earth floating like a boat in the blue ocean of ether. On all sides stretched mysteries, marvels, and prodigies, without limit, without number, and without change. I kissed the hem of the garments of God, and gave Him thanks for being Spirit, and being Life. Such moments are glimpses of the Divine, they make one conscious of eternity. They assure one that eternity itself is not too much for the study of the thoughts and works of the Eternal; they awake in us an adoring ecstasy, and the ardent humility of love."

The devout thought of these paragraphs passes in survey, first the EARTH (12–20); then the HEAVENS (21–26); and finally, the EXPERIENCE OF THE CHILDREN OF GOD in all ages (27–31).

(1) THE TESTIMONY OF THE EARTH.—It seems as though we are conducted to the shores of the Mediterranean, and stationed somewhere near the site of ancient Tyre. Before us spreads the Great Sea, as the Hebrews were wont to call it. Far across the waters, calm and tranquil, or heaving in memory of recent storms, sea and sky blend in the circle of the horizon. Now remember, says the prophet, God's hands are so strong and great that all that ocean and all other oceans lie in them as a drop on a man's palm. His fingers are so wide in their reach that their measure when outstretched can compass the breadth of heaven. His arms are so strong that they can hold balances and scales in which the loftiest mountains and the multitudinous isles of the Archipelago lie as small dust might do in the brass scales of a salesman. And this God is our God for ever and ever. He has taken not Israel only, but Jacob, into eternal union with Himself. The Creator of the ends of the earth is our Father. Creation is only one of his thoughts; but thou art his son, his heir, his beloved. See how careful He is of lilies and birds, of the delicate down on an insect's wing, and of the lichen traceries upon the stones. He cannot then fail thee, nor forsake thee.

Behind us lie the hills, and beyond them the mountains, and above them all Lebanon rears her snow-capped peaks like a bank of cumuli-clouds built up in the sky. But all the wood on Lebanon, its cedars riven with tempest and rugged with age, would not be too much to lay on the altar of Jehovah. And if all its beasts could be collected, and laid on the wood in sacrifice; and if Lebanon itself were the mighty altar of earth, there would be no extravagance in the vast burnt-offering that would fill the vault of heaven with fire and smoke. So great is God that the greatest gifts of human self-denial, which have cost men most, are not too great. How preposterous, therefore, it is to liken Him to any graven image or carving of wood! How needless to dread what men can do! How certain it is that He who spared not his own Son, but gave Him to a greater altar and fiercer flame, will with Him also freely give us all things!

All men may be in arms against thee, encircling thee with threats, and plotting to swallow thee up. But the nations are to Him as a drop of a bucket, and are counted as the small dust of the balance. The isles are very little things in his esteem, and their inhabitants as grasshoppers. Thou hast no reason therefore to be afraid. When thine enemies come upon thee, they shall stumble and fall. The Lord is thy Judge, thy Lawgiver, and thy King. He will save thee.

(2) THE TESTIMONY OF THE HEAVENS.—The scene shifts to the heavens, and all that is therein. With a marvellous prevision of the earth's circuit around the sun, Jehovah is depicted as sitting on the circle of its orbit, and looking thence on the populations of the earth. From that distance the teeming multitudes of mighty Babylon would seem insignificant enough, and there would be no appreciable difference between the monarch and the slave grinding at the mill. This is the antidote of fear. Sit in the heavenlies. Do not look from earth towards heaven, but from heaven towards earth. Let God, not man, be the standpoint of vision.

But this is not all. To this inspired thinker, it seemed as though the blue skies were curtains that God had stretched out as a housewife gauze (see R.V., marg.), or the fabric of a tent within which the pilgrim rests. If creation be His tent, which He fills in all its parts, how puny and pigmy are the greatest potentates of earth, "He bringeth princes to nothing, and maketh the judges of the earth as vanity." The child of God need not be abashed before the greatest of earthly rulers. Herod and Pontius Pilate, with the Gentiles, and all the people of Israel, may be gathered together; but they do whatsoever His hand and His counsel foreordained to come to pass. They are but stubble withered by the blast.

23

And even this is not all—day changes to night, and as the twilight deepens, the stars come out in their hosts; and suddenly, to the imagination of this lofty soul, the vault of heaven seems a pastureland over which a vast flock is following its Shepherd, who calls each by name. What a sublime conception, Jehovah, the Shepherd of the stars, leading them through space; conducting them with such care and might that none falls out of rank, or is lacking. And will Jehovah do so much for stars, and nought for sons? Will He not have a name for each? Will He not guide and guard each? Will He not see to it that none are lacking, when He brings his flock home at the end of the day? He who has kept the stars full of light for millenniums, and sustained them in their mighty rounds, will not do less for thee, his child. If thou wert reconciled to God by the death of his Son, thou wilt be surely saved by his life!

(3) THE TESTIMONY OF THE SAINTS.—Hast thou not heard? Where have been thine ears? This has not been told in secret, nor whispered in the dark places of the earth. It has been a commonplace with every generation of God's people, that the Lord fainteth-not, neither is weary. He never takes up a case to drop it. He never begins to build a character to leave it when it is half complete. He cannot be exhausted by the rebellion, backsliding, or fickleness of his children. Were this not so, heaven would have missed some of its noblest inhabitants. Jacob, David, Peter, and myriads more, are trophies of the unwearied pains which God takes with those whom He adopts into his family.

It is quite true that He may *seem* to forsake and to plunge the soul into needless trial; this, however, is no indication that He has tired of his charge, but only that He could not fulfil the highest blessedness of some soul He loved, save by sternest discipline. "There is no searching of his understanding."

There is another point on which all the saints are agreed, that neither weariness nor fainting are barriers to the forthputting of God's might. On the contrary, they possess an infinite attractiveness to his nature. We have seen a little weakling child draw to its cot some strong and burly man, the champion athlete of the countryside. Such a spell can weakness exert over might, and helplessness

24

over helpfulness. It is the burden of Scripture that the strong should bear the infirmities of the weak, and not please themselves. Such is the law of God's existence. All that He is and has He holds in trust for us, and most for those who need most.

In point of fact, many of us are too strong, self-reliant, and resouceful to get the best that God can do. Wait a little, till thy strength begins to faint beneath the burdens and the noon-tide heat, till the energy that was thy boast has slowly ebbed away, and thou art left without might. Then the Mighty One of Jacob will draw nigh thee, and impart both power and strength. Jacob must halt on his thigh ere he can prevail with God and man.

They that *wait* on God, *renew* their strength. It is new strength for each new duty and trial. As each fresh demand is made on them they receive some fresh baptism, some unrealised enduement. Ah, happy art, nearly forgotten in these busy days! Nothing, not even youthful genius and vigour, can be a substitute for this!

The gradation is a remarkable one. At first sight it would appear that it should pass from walking to running, and from this to flying ; but the order is reversed, as though it were easier to mount with wings than walk without fainting. And so, indeed it is. Any racehorse will start at full speed ; but how few have staying power! The tyro in cycling will go at full pelt ; but only the experienced rider can walk or stand. To pursue the common track of daily duty—not faltering nor growing weary—to do so when novelty has worn off, when the elasticity of youth has vanished, when the applause of the crowd has become dim and faint—this is the greatest achievement of the Christian life. For this earthly and human strength will not avail. But God is all-sufficient. Never faint or weary Himself, He is able to infuse such resistless energy into the soul that waits on Him, that if it mounts, it shall be on eagle-wing ; if it runs, it will not weary ; if it walks, it will not faint.

4

THE CONVOCATION OF THE NATIONS

"Triumphant Faith!
Who from the distant earth looks up to heaven,
Seeing indivisibility suspending
Eternity from the breath of God.
Lo! with step erect
She walks o'er whirlpool waves and martyr fires,
And depths of darkness and chaotic voids."

E. Tatham

(Isaiah 41:1)

The conception of this passage is superb. Jehovah is represented as summoning the earth, as far as the remote isles of the west, to determine once and for ever who is the true God: whether He, or the idols and oracles of which there were myriads worshipped and believed in by every nation under heaven.

The test proposed is a very simple one. The gods of the nations were to predict events in the near future, or to show that they had had a clear understanding of the events of former days. "Produce your cause, saith the Lord; bring forth your strong reasons, saith the King of Jacob. Let them bring them forth, and declare unto us what shall happen; declare ye the former things, what they be, that we may consider them, and know the latter end of them; or show us things for to come." On the other hand, the servant of Jehovah was prepared to show how fast-sealed prophecies, committed to the custody of his race, had been precisely verified in the event, and to utter minute predictions about Cyrus, "the one from the East," which should be fulfilled before that generation had passed away. Not, as in Elijah's case, would the appeal be made to the descending flame; but to the fitting of prophecy and historical fact.

Immediately there is a great commotion, the isles see

and fear, the ends of the earth tremble, they draw near and come to the Judgment-seat. On the way thither each bids the other take courage. There is an industrious furbishing up of the dilapidated idols, and manufacturing of new ones. The carpenter encourages the goldsmith; and he that smooths with the hammer him that smites the anvil. They examine the soldering to see if it will stand, and drive great nails to render the idols steadfast. The universal desire is to make a strong set of gods who will be able to meet the Divine challenge—much as if a Roman Catholic priest were to regild and repaint images of the saints on the time-worn altar of a fishing hamlet, in the hope of securing from them greater help in quelling the winter storms.

History furnishes some interesting confirmations of this contrast between the predictions of heathen oracles and the clear prophecies of Old Testament Scripture, which were so literally and minutely realised. For instance, Herodotus tells us that when Crœsus heard of the growing power of Cyrus, he was so alarmed for his kingdom, that he sent rich presents to the oracles at Delphi, Dodona, and elsewhere, asking what would be the outcome of his victorious march. That at Delphi gave this ambiguous reply, "That he would destroy a great empire," but whether the empire would be that of Cyrus or of Crœsus was left unexplained: thus, which ever way the event turned, the oracle could claim to have predicted it. This is a fair illustration of the manner in which the oracles answered the appeals made to them by men or nations when in the agony of fear. How striking a contrast the precise prediction of these pages, which give us the name of the conqueror; the quarter from which he would fall upon Babylon; the marvellous series of successes, that gave kings as dust to his sword, and as the driven stubble to his bow; his reverence towards God, his simplicity and integrity of purpose (verses 2, 3, 25; 45:1).

We are learning to lay increasing stress on prophecy. What miracles were to a former age, the predicitions of the Bible are to this; and, unlike the miracles, the evidence of prophecy becomes stronger with every century that passes between its first utterance and its fulfilment. Probably there is an unrealised wealth of attestation lying in the ancient records of Egypt and Babylon, which is on

27

the eve of being made available against the attacks of infidelity.

How sad, on the other hand, it is to mark the trend of opinion, in quarters where we should least expect it, towards the muttering of oracle and the whispering of familiar spirits; the rehabilitation of that lying system which filled the world at the incarnation of Christ, but which Milton at least supposed had for ever vanished before the rising beams of the Sun of Righteousness.

> *"So when the sun in bed,*
> *Curtained with cloudy red,*
> *Pillows his chin upon an Orient wave,*
> *The flocking shadows pale*
> *Troop to the infernal jail,*
> *Each fetter'd ghost slips to his several grave;*
> *And the yellow skirted fayes*
> *Fly after the night-steed, leaving their moon-loved maze."*

Amidst the excitement of this vast convocation the idols are dumb. We can almost see them borne into the arena by their attendant priests, resplendent in gold and tinsel, flashing with jewels, bedizened in gorgeous apparel. They are set in a row, their acolytes swing high the censer, the monotonous drawl of their votaries arises in supplication. Silence is proclaimed, that they may have an opportunity of pronouncing on the subject submitted to them; but they are speechless. Jehovah pronounces the verdict against which there can be no appeal, "Behold, ye are of nothing and your work of nought: an abomination is he that chooseth you" (verse 24). As Jehovah looks, there is no one. When He asks of them, there is no counsellor that can answer a word. "Behold they are all vanity; their works are nought; their molten images are wind and confusion."

Whilst this great cause is being decided, the people of God are addressed in words of tender comfort, which are as fresh and life-giving to-day as when first spoken by lip, or written by pen.

(1) THE CIRCUMSTANCES IN WHICH GOD ADDRESSES HIS PEOPLE.—They are poor and needy; they seek water, and there is none; the heights are bare, and the valleys

verdureless; the track of their life lies through the wilderness; they are surrounded by incensed enemies who strive with them; they are powerless as a worm. It is amongst such that God has always found his chosen. Not the wise and prudent, but the babes; not the high and mighty, but the lowly and obscure; not the king, but the shepherd-lad; not Eli, but Samuel. He finds them in their low estate, cast aside and disowned by the world, and adopting them, He makes for Himself a name and a praise.

It is necessary that God should have room in which to work. Emptiness to receive Him; weakness to be empowered by Him. It is into the empty branch that the vine sap pours; to the hollowed basin that the water flows; the weakness of the child gives scope for the man's strength. The need of the countless multitudes that thronged Christ's earthly life gave Him opportunity for the working of his miracles, and the putting forth of his power. The lower the platform, the greater the proof of what God can be and do to those who trust Him. Take heart, therefore, if thou canst discover thyself in any of those that are summoned to thy view by the enumeration of want, and weariness, and sin. The prime blessedness of the kingdom of heaven is for the poor in spirit, the persecuted and the tempted, the wandering sheep, and the famishing child.

(2) THE ASSURANCES THAT HE MAKES TO THEM.—No height, however bare, nor depth, however profound, can separate us from his love. He whispers, amid the gloom that has settled down upon the landscape of our life, "Fear thou not, for I am with thee." No enemies, however numerous or enraged, need dismay us; for He is still our God, bound to us by covenant relationship, able to throw reinforcements into the citadel of our heart, succouring us with horses and chariots of fire. Heart and flesh may fail; but He will strengthen. Difficulties may seem insurmountable; but He will help. The feet may be cut and bleeding with the desert march; but He will uphold with his strong right hand (13, 14).

There is a striking passage in one of the psalms which dilates with all the pride of the Jew-patriot upon the glories of Jerusalem, the city of the great King, in which God had made Himself known as a refuge. The kings of the nations, intent upon her destruction, assemble

29

themselves and pass by her frowning battlements; but as they see the inviolable protection of God flung around them, they are dismayed, trembling takes hold of them, and they haste away. So, when strong enemies threaten the life, the purity, the well-being of God's elect, He flings around them so complete and inviolable a defence that foes become as nothing, and as a thing of nought. And the beleaguered soul entrenched within its strong fortifications is reassured by the repeated refrain of Jehovah's voice, "Fear not; I will help thee."

And when God sets his hand to save any of his saints, He does not stay with this; but goes on to use the saved one for the blessing of others. Hence He not only comforts the few men of Israel with the assurance of his ready help, reiterating the words, as though never weary of repeating them; but He promises to make of them, worms though they were, a new sharp threshing instrument, having teeth which would thresh the mountains and beat them small, and make the hills as chaff. This prediction has been marvellously fulfilled in the history of the Jewish nation, which has exercised such a formative influence on the history of the world; and there is a similar experience awaiting all who will surrender themselves absolutely to the hands of God. In thine own estimation thou mayest be nothing more than a worm; yet if thou dost yield thyself absolutely to God, He will make thee a new sharp threshing instrument having teeth (15, 16).

Who is there that does not long to be renewed, to have a fresh baptism, a fresh beginning in work and energy of life? Who is there that does not wish to be delivered from the bluntness and obtuseness which comes from long use? Who is there that does not desire power to thresh the mountains of sin and evil, until they are dissipated like the heaps of chaff on the threshing-floor before the evening breeze? Let such take to their comfort the assertion of Jehovah, *"I will make."* There is nothing that thou canst not do, O worm of a man, if Jehovah, thy Redeemer, the Holy One, takes thee in hand.

(3) THE DIVINE PROVISION FOR THEIR NEED.—Life is not easy for any of us, if we regard the external conditions only; but directly we learn the Divine secret, rivers flow over bare heights in magnificent cascades; fountains arise

in the rock-strewn sterile valleys; the wilderness becomes a pool, and the dry land springs; the plain is covered with noble trees, and the desert with the beautiful undergrowth of a forest-glade (17, 18).

To the ordinary eye it is probable that there would appear no difference. Still the tiny garret, and the wasting illness; still the pining child, with its low moan of continued pain; still the monotony and lovelessness of a lonely desolate life; still the straitened circumstances— still the deferred hope. But the eye of faith beholds a paradise of beauty, murmuring brooks filling the air with melody, leafy trees spreading their shade.

What makes the difference? What does faith see? How is she able to make such transformations?

(1) Faith is conscious that God is there, and that his presence is the complement of every need. To her eye common desert bushes burn with his shekinah.

(2) Faith recognises the reality of an eternal choice, that God has entered into a covenant which cannot be dissolved, and that his love and fidelity are bound to finish the work He has commenced.

(3) Faith knows that there is a loving purpose running through every moment of trial, and that the Great Refiner has a meaning in every degree of heat to which the furnace is raised: and she anticipates the moment when she will see what God has foreseen all the time, and towards which He has been working.

(4) Faith realises that others are learning from her experiences lessons which nothing else would teach them; and that glory is accruing to God in the highest, because men and angels see and know and consider and understand together that the hand of the Lord hath done this, and the Holy One of Israel hath created it (20).

Some readers of these words may be wearily traversing the wilderness in their daily experience. They seek water, and there is none; and their tongue faileth for thirst. But if only they would look up with the eyes of faith, they would behold, as Hagar did, wells of water, and the fertility of the Land of Beulah. Many pilgrims pass through that land and see nothing like what Bunyan describes—no sun shines for them; nor birds sing; nor ravishing beauty charms the sense. These entrancing delights are all around; but they are unseen, unknown. While others find paradise in the unlikeliest surroundings. The

31

difference between these experiences arises from the presence or absence of the faith that takes

> *". . . true measure*
> *Of its eternal treasure."*

Therefore comfort thy heart. Wait patiently. Let faith have her way. Hope to the end for the grace to be brought unto thee. Ponder these things till, in thy case also, what seems only a desert to other eyes, to thine shall be as the garden of the Lord.

5

"BEHOLD MY SERVANT"

> *"He does not fail*
> *For thy impatience, but stands by thee still;*
> *Patient, unfaltering—till thou too shalt grow*
> *Patient,—and wouldst not miss the sharpness grown*
> *To custom, which assures Him at thy side."*

H. Hamilton King

(Isaiah 42:1)

When our Lord took on Himself the form of a servant, girded Himself, and began to wash the feet of his disciples, it was no new office that He performed; for the life of God is ever one of service, of ministry. He rules all, because He serves all. Inasmuch as He is the highest, He must also be the lowliest, according to the everlasting order of the spiritual realm. The ministry of Jesus was therefore the revelation of the life that God had ever been living in the blue depths of heaven; and if once we can learn the principles of that life which filled hundreds and thousands of homes with blessing and joy during those marvellous years of earthly ministry, we shall have a model on which to form our own service to God and man. Our Lord's life and ministry revealed the ideal of service.

There is no doubt as to the applicability of this passage to our Lord. The Holy Ghost, by the evangelist Matthew, directly refers it to Him, and says its meaning was filled to the brim by that matchless life which for a brief space cast its radiance on our world (Matt. 12:18). Oh that He who took upon Him the form of a servant—who was amongst his disciples as one that served, and who proposes some day to wait on his wearied workers as they sit together at his table in his kingdom—may so incarnate Himself in us, that we in our measure may repeat those features of his earthly ministry, which God can crown with the enduement of his Holy Spirit, and with which He can co-operate! "I have put my Spirit upon Him." "I will hold thine hand."

They are rare qualities which Jehovah calls us to behold in the elect Servant in whom his soul delights: a Divine modesty ; a Divine humility ; a Divine perseverance.

(1) THE MODESTY OF THE BEST WORK.—God is always at work in our world, leading the progress of suns, refreshing grass with dew, directing the flight of the morning beams, and the glancing light of the firefly ; compassing our path and our lying down, and determining the fall of the shell on the sand of the ocean bottom. But all his work is done so quietly, so unobtrusively, with such reticence as to his personal agency, that many affirm there is no God at all.

He spreads the breakfast table each morning for myriads in wood, and ocean, and the homes of men ; but steals away before we catch sight of Him to whom we owe all. We know that He has been at work ; but He is gone without a sound, without a footmark, leaving only the evident touch of his hand.

Thus it was with the work of Christ. He put his hand on the mouths of those who proclaimed his deity, or blazoned abroad his fame. He repeatedly told the recipients of his bounty that they must not make Him known. He stole away from the multitudes that filled the porches of Bethesda ; so that the healed paralytic wist not who had healed him. He lingered as long as He could in the highlands of Galilee, until his brethren remonstrated with Him. He did not strive, nor cry, nor lift up, nor cause his voice to be heard in the street.

This quality is God's hall-mark upon the best work.

His highest artists do not inscribe their names upon their pictures, nor introduce their portraits amongst their groups. It is enough for them to have borne witness to the truth and beauty of the universe ; they wish for nothing more than to reveal what they have seen in nature's holiest shrines, or in the transient gleams of beauty in the human face. To win a soul for God ; to cleanse the scar of the leper ; to make blind eyes see ; to give back the dead to mother, sister, friend—this is recompense enough. To look up from the accomplished work into the face of God ; to catch his answering smile ; to receive the reward of the Father who is in secret—this is heaven, compared with which the praise of man is as valueless as his censure.

Art thou conscious, fellow servant, that this is the temper of thy soul, the quality of thy work? For if not, if in thy secret soul thou seekest the sweet voice of human adulation, if thou art conscious of a wish to pass the results of thy work into newspaper paragraph or to common talk of men, be sure that deterioration is fast corrupting thy service, as rottenness the autumn fruit. It is high time that thou shouldest withdraw thyself to some lonely spot, where the silt that darkens the crystal waters of thy soul may drop away, and again they mirror nothing but the sky with its depths of blue, its hosts of stars. The only work that God approves, that is permanent and fruitful, that partakes of the nature of Christ, is that which neither seeks nor needs advertisement. The bird is content to sing ; the flower to be beautiful ; the child to unfold its nature to the eye of love ; and the true worker to do the will of God.

(2) THE HUMILITY OF THE BEST WORK.—God's choicest dealings have been with shepherd boys taken freshly from their flocks ; with youngest sons without repute ; with maidens growing to mature beauty in the obscurity of some highland village. He has put down the mighty from their seat, and exalted the humble and meek. And so was it with our Lord. He passed by Herod's palace, and chose Bethlehem and its manger bed. He refused the empires of the world, and took the way of the cross. He selected his apostles and disciples from the ranks of the poor. He revealed his choicest secrets to babes. He left the society of the Pharisee and Scribe, and expended

Himself on bruised reeds and smoking flax, on dying thieves and fallen women, and the peasantry of Galilee.

A reed! How typical it is of the broken heart crushed by the tread of unkindness and tyranny! There is no beauty in its russet plume. There is no strength in its slender stem. There is no attractiveness in the fever-breeding swamp where it grows. And if none would journey far in search of a reed, how much less of one that had been crushed by the boisterous frolic of the river-horse, or by the tread of the peasant! So hearts get broken. Too fragile to resist the pressure of the mad rush of selfishness and the tread of unfeeling cruelty, without a sound they break, and thenceforth are cast aside as some useless thing, not worth a thought.

The smoking flax! How it smoulders! How slowly the sparks follow one another along its fibres! How powerless it is to kindle the slightest gauze to a flame! So feebly does love burn in some hearts, that only He who knows all things can know that love is there at all. So fitful, so irregular, so destitute of kindling power. Ah me! reader, you and I have known hours when not the coals of juniper, but the smoking flax, have been the true emblem of our love.

The superficial worker ignores these in rude haste. He passes them by to seek an object more commensurate with his powers. Give me, he cries, a sphere in which I may influence strong, noble, and heroic souls! Give me an arena where I may meet foemen worthy of my steel! Give me a task where my stores of knowledge may have adequate scope! And if these fail, he counts himself ill-used. "I will do nought, if I cannot do the best." Oh, foolish words! The best, the noblest, is to bend with a Divine humility over those whom the world ignores, exercising a holy ingenuity, a sacred inventiveness; making of bruised reeds pipes of music or measuring rods for the New Jerusalem; fanning the spark of the smoking flax until that which had nearly died out in the heart of a Peter, sets on fire three thousand souls within seven weeks of its threatened extinction.

This is also the test of true work. Where does it find thee, fellow-worker? Art thou ambitious for a larger sphere; grudging the pains needed to explain the gospel to the ignorant; to cope with the constant relapses and

35

backslidings of the weak ; to combat the fears of the timorous and mistrustful ; to adjust the perpetual disputes and quarrellings of new-made disciples ; to suit thy pace to the weakest and youngest of the flock? Beware! Thy work is in danger of losing its noblest quality ; the hue is passing off the summer fruit ; the tender tone which God loves is fading from thy picture ; the grace of the day is dying. Before it is too late, get alone with God to learn that the noblest souls are sometimes found within bruised bodies, and the greatest work often emanates from the most inconspicuous sparks.

(3) DIVINE PERSEVERANCE.—Though our Lord is principally concerned with the bruised and the dimly-burning wick, He is neither one nor the other (see R.V., marg.). He is neither discouraged nor does He fail. In the primeval world, the successive platforms on which He wrought in the ascending scale of creation were perpetually submerged by waves of chaos that swept them clear of his handiwork ; but through all He persevered until the heavens and earth which now exist stood forth apparelled in beauty that elicited from the lips of the Creator the verdict, "It is very good." Thus it shall be in the spiritual world. The centuries which have followed on Calvary's supreme sacrifice have witnessed alterations of chaos with cosmos ; of disorder with order ; of confusion with advancing civilization. In the eighth, ninth, and tenth centuries especially, it seemed as though the results of the tears and martyrdoms and witnessing of the earlier age were entirely lost. But the Master was never once discouraged, nor slacked his hand ; but through good report and evil pursued his purpose.

This again, is the quality of the best work. That which emanates from the flesh is full of passion, fury, and impulse. It essays to deliver Israel by a spasm of force that lays an Egyptian dead in the sand ; but it soon exhausts itself, and sinks back nerveless and spent. The renunciation of an enterprise, undertaken in hot haste, proves that it was assumed in the energy of the flesh, not given by the suggestion of the Spirit. Perseverance in the face of scorn and difficulty—in the teeth of pitiless criticism and obstinate hate, up the hill-brow, or across the trembling quag—is a proof that the task has been Divinely given, and that the ardent soul is feeding its strength from the Divine resources. If this perseverance is failing thee, bethink thee whether thy task is Heaven's or of thine own choosing; if the latter, abandon it; but if indeed the former, then wait on the Lord till thy strength is renewed, and thou, too, shalt neither be discouraged nor fail.

But qualities like these, however excellent, cannot avail, with us, at least, until there has been added, *the enduement of the Holy Ghost.* "I will put my Spirit upon Him." At the waters of baptism that promise was fulfilled; for as the Lord emerged from them, the heavens were opened, and the Spirit in a bodily shape descended upon Him and abode. Then his mouth was opened, and his public ministry commenced. For thirty years He had been content with the obscure and contemplative life of Nazareth; now He stepped forth into the world saying, "The Spirit of the Lord God is upon Me, and He has anointed Me to preach."

What that scene was in the life of the Lord, Pentecost was for the Church. Then she was anointed for her Divine mission among men; the unction of the Holy One rested upon her, to be continued and renewed as the centuries slowly passed. What happened for the Church should take place in the history of each member of it. This anointing is for all, is to be received by faith, and is specially intended to equip us for work. Hast thou had thy share? If not, art thou not making a mistake in attempting God's work without it? Tarry till thou art endued. Hast thou known it? Seek it on the threshold of each new enterprise. Be satisfied with nothing less than to be anointed with fresh oil.

And even this is not all. In the words, "I will hold thy hand and keep thee," a suggestion is made of the co-operation of the Holy Ghost with every true servant of God. As we begin to speak, He falls on them that hear the Word. As we witness to the death, resurrection, and glory of Jesus, He witnesses also to the conscience and heart. When the voice from heaven speaks by our lips, the Holy Spirit says, Yea. Thus all the words of God through us receive the demonstration of the Holy Spirit, as though one were to demonstrate by experiments, optically, what a lecturer was expounding orally to the ear of his audience.

It is impossible too strongly to emphasise the necessity of relying in Christian work on the co-witness of the Spirit of God. It not only relieves the worker of undue and exhausting strain by dividing his responsibilities with his Divine Partner ; but it reinforces him with immeasurable power. This is what the apostle means by "the communion of the Holy Ghost," which signifies the having in common. Happy is he who has learnt such community of aim and method with the Divine Spirit, as to be able to derive the greatest possible assistance from his co-operation.

Such are the Divine principles of service ; and they need to be studied by each of us, if we would hear God say of us, in our measure, "Behold my servant whom I uphold ; mine elect, in whom my soul delighteth."

6

"YE ARE MY WITNESSES"

"Out of that weak, unquiet drift,
That comes but to depart,
To that pure Heaven my spirit lift
Where Thou unchanging art!
Thy purpose of eternal good
Let me but surely know:
On this I'll lean, let changing mood
And feeling come or go!"

J. Campbell Sharp

(Isaiah 43 : 10)

The magnificent conception with which chapter 41 opens underlies this. We have still the vast convocation of the world, summoned to decide whether Jehovah, or some idol god, should henceforth be regarded as the supreme Deity. In the arena are the rows of helpless images, rich in paint and tinsel, but mute, only waiting to be carried home by their attendant priests. Before the assembly disperses, Jehovah must vindicate his claims ; and therefore calls into the witness-box his chosen people, that they may tell men what they know, and testify what they have seen.

It is a remarkable appeal. In chapter 42:19 they are blamed for being blind and deaf; but for all that they are addressed as capable of giving evidence. Though they had misused their opportunities, and had made less progress than they might have done in the knowledge of God, yet they knew more of Him than any nation beside upon the face of the earth, and could tell secrets which the profoundest thinkers had missed. "Ye are My witnesses, and My servant whom I have chosen."

See, they come into court and take their stand face to face with monarchies that had ruthlessly despoiled and ravaged them, to speak for Him whose character had been so often maligned and misrepresented by their sins. At the period in which they were summoned to give evidence, they were actually in captivity, diminished in numbers, brought low through affliction and oppression; and yet, such is the power of witness to truth, their testimony was to silence all other voices; to bear down all rival claims; and to establish Jehovah as the one and only God. They might be vanquished and broken in the realm of physical force; but they were supreme and imperial in the realm of truth. Thus, in after days, the Lord Jesus stood bound before the representative of mighty Rome, bearing witness to a Kingdom which did not emanate from this world, but before which that of Rome was to pass into the land of shadows.

See, then, the Jews enter the arena, carrying with them their venerable sacred books. The test, as we have seen, being whether Jehovah had uttered predictions which had been fulfilled.

"Has your God foretold the future?"

"Certainly!" they reply.

"Give some instances."

"In our oldest record, centuries before it took place, He told our ancestor and progenitor Abraham, that his descendants would spend a protracted period in Egyptian bondage; and that afterwards they should come forth amid great judgments, to inhabit the land in which he was a stranger. This was precisely fulfilled.

"Again, Jehovah foretold that Hagar's son, Ishmael, should be as a wild ass, at feud with all his neighbours. This, too, has been realised in the history of Edom.

"Again, through his prophet Isaiah, on the fatal day when our great king Hezekiah showed the ambassadors of the king of Babylon his treasures, Jehovah foretold that we should be captives in this land, and our princes chamberlains in the palace of our conqueror—as it is this day."

The Jews have maintained this witness through the ages. Think of Babylon to-day, wrapt in the sand-drifts in the desert. No Arab pitches his tent there, neither do shepherds fold their flocks. It is the haunt of wild beasts, a possession for the bittern, and a dwelling-place for dragons. Think of Tyre, on whose site a few fisher-folk get a scanty livelihood, drying their nets on its ruins; whilst the noble harbour in which, when Nahum wrote, the wealth of the world proudly floated, is choked up with sand. Think of Edom, from whose rock-hewn houses, situated in vast solitudes and seldom visited by man, arise vast flocks of birds, which almost darken the air at the approach of a stranger. No unprejudiced mind could compare the condition of these sites with the predictions of the Old Testament, without being impressed with their strong evidence to the truth of Scripture.

The very existence of the Jewish people scattered throughout the world, and yet preserved from absorption amid the populations that surround them—that they have no rest for the sole of their foot; that they have a trembling heart, and failing of eyes, and pining of soul; that they fear night and day, and have none assurance of life; that they are evidently being kept for their land, as their land is being kept for them—all this is in exact conformity to the words of Moses in the Book of Deuteronomy.

The special function of witness-bearing for God is not, however, confined to the Jewish people; but by the express words of the Lord it is shared by the Church. The Church and the Holy Spirit together bear joint witness to the death, resurrection, and eternal life of the Divine Man. "Ye shall be My witnesses, both in Jerusalem and in all Judæa and Samaria, and unto the uttermost parts of the earth." As the King bore witness to the truth, his subjects bear witness to the truth as it is in Jesus. When his matchless life set from the eye of men behind Calvary, the Church, illumined by fellowship with Him across the spaces which no mortal eye can fathom, testified that He lived for evermore. It may be said of her, as the psalmist did of the heavenly bodies, Day unto day she uttereth speech, night unto night showeth knowledge. There is no speech or utterance, her voice cannot be heard; but her line is gone out through all the earth, and her words to the end of the world.

This is also the function of the individual believer; not to argue and dispute, not to demonstrate and prove, not to perform the part of the advocate; but to live in direct contact with things which the Holy Ghost reveals to the pure and childlike nature. And then to come forth attesting that these things are so. Just as mathematical axioms have no need to be argued, but simply to be stated, and the statement is sufficient to establish them, because of the affinity between them and the construction of the human mind; so it is sufficient to bear witness to truth, amid systems of falsehood and error. And directly it is uttered, there is an assent in the conscience illumined by the Holy Spirit, which rises up and declares it to be the very truth of God.

There are three points on which the Christian soul is called to give witness. They are suggested by the glowing words of which this call for witnesses is the climax; and we need have no hesitation in appropriating such words—addressed primarily to the Jews—to ourselves, because we are so distinctly told that we are no longer strangers from the covenant of promise, but are part of the household of God (Eph. 2:12–19). It is also affirmed by the apostle that those which be of faith are blessed with faithful Abraham, and that the blessing of Abraham in Christ Jesus comes upon the Gentiles (Gal. 3:9–14).

(1) LET US WITNESS TO A LOVE THAT NEVER TIRES.—At the close of the previous chapter we have a terrible picture of Israel as a people robbed and spoiled, snared in holes, and hid in prison-houses; upon whom God was pouring the fury of his anger, and the strength of battle. Then most unexpectedly God turns to them, and says, "Fear not! thou art mine; thou hast been precious in my sight, and honourable and beloved."

Thou art mine. The words are very simple. They would come to a little lost child from a mother's lips as she again embraced it. Our deepest emotions express themselves in the simplest words. Depth and intensity of feeling

41

select the monosyllables of the mother-tongue. It is much for thee, O exiled soul, robbed and spoiled, that God still calls thee his; and He will not stay his hand until He elicits the response, "Great and Good God, Thou art mine!" Neither sin nor sorrow can cut with their accursed shears the knot of union which the Divine fingers have tied between thy weak soul and the everlasting Lover of men.

Precious. Israel hardly dared to think it; and certainly no observer unacquainted with the ways of God could dare suppose that Jehovah counted his people as his priceless treasure. But, nevertheless, the words stand out clearly upon the page, "Thou hast been *precious* in My sight." Yes, soul of man, thou art the pearl of great price to obtain which the merchantman in search of priceless jewels sold all that He had, and bought the world in which thou didst lie like a common pebble. Preciousness is due to hardships undergone, purchase money and time expended, or pains of workmanship; and each of these three conditions has been marvellously exemplified in the dealings of thy God.

Honourable. Our origin was in the dust. Our father was an Amorite, our mother a Hittite. In the day of our birth none pitied; but we were cast out in the open field and abhorred. It is marvellous to know that God is prepared to raise such out of the dust and lift them from the dunghill; to make them sit with princes, and inherit the throne of glory. Ah! how little do the titles of the world appear to those whom God dubs "right honourable"! On them the loftiest angels are proud to wait. Their nursing-fathers are kings. Demean thyself as one whom God delights to honour. It ill-becomes princes of the blood-royal to lie in the gutter.

Beloved. "I have loved thee." These are words which no explanation is needed to elucidate. We must sit down to muse on them, and let their quiet influence steal over us, like that of a superb painting, a strain of music, a landscape. But oh, believe them; and in the darkest hours of life, when thy feet have almost gone from under thee, and no sun, or moon, or stars appear, never doubt that God's love is not less tenacious than that which suggested the epitaph on Kingsley's tomb, "We love; we have loved; we will love."

To know all this, and to bear witness to it; to attest it in the teeth of adverse circumstances, of bitter taunts, and of utter desolation; to persist in the affirmation amid the cross-questioning of a cynical age; never to falter, never to listen to the suggestion of doubt rising like a cold mist to enwrap the soul; never to allow the expression of the face to suggest that God is hard in his dealings —this is the mission of the believer.

(2) LET US WITNESS TO A PURPOSE THAT NEVER FALTERS. —God does not say, "Think of what was done yesterday"; He goes back on the purposes of eternity; the deeds of Bethlehem and Calvary; the everlasting covenant; the whole trend of his dealings with us. He says, "Read the whole book; step back and consider the perspective; get a glimpse of the mighty roots that moor the slight tree of thy life." "Fear not! for I have redeemed thee; I have. called thee by thy name; I have created thee for my glory; I have formed thee, yea, I have made thee" (verses 1, 7).

Is it likely that a purpose reaching back into the blue azure of the past will be lightly dropped? The love of yesterday may pass, as the dew from the earth; the hastily formed purpose may be as hastily abandoned; the gourd of the night perishes in the night; but thine election is the outworking of an ideal which filled the mind of God before ever the sun began to glimmer, or seraph's voice to strike across the depths of the infinite.

This, too, demands our witness. Men misjudge God, because they look at his work in fragments, and criticise half-finished designs. Short-sighted, premature, hasty, the adverse criticism of man must be corrected by the mature, calm judgment which shall view the finished scheme of creation and of the moral government of the universe. It is our duty to appeal for this, and bear our witness to the far-reach of a purpose that moves in a slowly-ascending spiral to its end.

(3) LET US WITNESS TO A DELIVERANCE THAT NEVER DIS-APPOINTS.—God does not keep his children from the waters and the fire. We might have expected the verse would run, "Thou shalt never pass through the waters, or through the river; thou shalt never have to walk through the fire!" But so far from this, it seems taken

43

as a matter of course that there will be the waters and the fire; the overflowing floods of sorrow; the biting flame of sarcasm and hate. God's people are not saved from trial, but in it. Fire and water and cleansing agents that cannot be dispensed with. The gold and silver, the brass, iron, and tin, everything that can abide the fire, must go through the fire, that it may be clean; and that which cannot abide the fire must go through the water (Num. 31 : 23).

Sometimes the world wonders at seeing God's people in trouble as other men—not knowing that the King Himself has passed through flood and flame; not knowing also that there are fords for the floods and paths through the fire. God does not take us to the city that hath foundations by a way which will mock our faltering footsteps. We must bear our testimony to this also, that we may clear the character of God from the aspersions of the ungodly. He will not break the silence to speak for Himself; but we must bear witness for Him.

The witness-box is the home, the place of business, the society salon, anywhere and everywhere where the right is being travestied and misunderstood. There, in the power of the witnessing Spirit, we are called to be witnesses for the Lord our God."

7

THE ALTERING OF GOD'S PURPOSE

"To the spirit select there is no choice;
He cannot say, This will I do, or that.
  . . . . .
A hand is stretched to him from out the dark,
Which grasping without question, he is led
Where there is work that he must do for God."

Lowell

(Isaiah 43:21)

This refers primarily to Israel. It is the burden of the Book of Deuteronomy, that God chose the seed of Abraham to be a peculiar nation unto Himself, above all peoples on the face of the earth. It was for this He brought them out from Egypt, the house of bondage, and separated them amid the highlands of Canaan. They were to be his own inheritance. Those two words, *people* and *inheritance,* are perpetually linked together in the Bible. "The Lord hath taken you, and brought you forth out of the iron furnace, out of Egypt, to be unto Him a people of inheritance as at this day." It was as though He viewed his people as a plot of land, which after careful tendance would yield to Him crop after crop of delight (Deut. 4:20; 7:6).

In his swan-song, the great lawgiver went so far as to say that when the Most High gave the nations their inheritance, He apportioned their lot, and fixed their bounds with reference to the nation which was as the apple of his eye. Thus a market-gardener will separate a few choice plants, and concentrate on them his most eager attention—not for their sakes alone; but that he may procure seed and slips to sow and plant over all the acres that belong to him. "The Lord's portion is his people; Jacob is the lot of his inheritance" (Deut. 32:9).

Jehovah's design is clearly declared in the significant passage that heads this chapter—"They shall show forth

My praise." By a long process of careful training, it was his intention so to form the people that their history should turn men's thoughts to the glory and beauty of his own nature, and elicit perpetual adoration and praise. They were to go forth throughout the world teaching men the love and goodness of Him who had found them in the waste howling wilderness, a race of untutored slaves, and had made them a nation of priests, of sweet psalmists, and of seers proclaiming the transcendant beauty of the only God. By repeated failure the Jews set themselves against the accomplishment of the Divine plan. On three separate occasions they thwarted Jehovah. They came nigh unto cursing instead of praising. They gave men false conceptions of his character. And on three separate occasions they had to learn the temporary suspension and postponement of his purpose (Num. 14:34).

First, in the wilderness they murmured against Him, and were sent back to wander in the waste for forty years. Next, after nineteen kings had ruled from David's throne, they were exiled to Babylon for seventy years. And lastly, since the rejection of the Beloved Son, they have been driven into all the world, to be a by-word and a proverb. For eighteen hundred years God's purpose has been under arrest. It shall, no doubt, be ultimately fulfilled. The chosen people shall yet be for a name, for a praise, and for a glory; but in the meanwhile the Gentiles have been called in to take their place, temporarily indeed, but with blessed results for them, until the branches which were broken off are again grafted into their olive-tree, and all Israel shall be saved (Jer 13:11; Rom. 11:23).

This change of purpose on the part of God has been the opening of the door for us; and the words which were originally addressed to Israel are now applicable to ourselves. Twice at least in the epistles, and by the lips of the apostles, Paul and Peter, we are told that Jesus gave Himself for us, to redeem us and to purify us unto Himself, a people for his own possession; so that we are an elect race, a royal priesthood, a holy nation, a people for God's own possession, that we may show forth the praises of Him who called us out of darkness into his marvellous light. We are what we are, that we may show forth God's praise; but if we fail to realise his ideal, for us too there will be the inevitable postponement of his

46

purpose. Instead of being realised easily and blessedly, it will be wrought out, as has repeatedly been the case with Israel, through tears and blood (Titus 2:14; 1 Peter 2:9).

(1) THE PURPOSE OF GOD.—"That they should show forth My praise." It has been said that the word translated *praise* is from the same root as *Hallel* in "Hallelujah"; and that it means, first, a clear and shining light; next, a sweet flute-like sound; from which we learn that the people of God are to reflect his glory until it shines from their lives, attracting others to it; and that they are to speak his praise in resonant and harmonious sounds that shall arrest and attract the listening ear. "How fair He must be whose service has filled these souls with such delight! Come, let us seek Him, that He may do as much for us!"

We may promote God's praise by suffering, as much as by active service. To lie still day after day, without complaining—satisfied with what pleases Him, and resolute to suffer according to the will of God, though no word fall from our lips—may be more provocative of praise, than to write psalms which stir successive generations to praise and bless Him whose mercy endureth for ever.

In every life there are three regions. That of the light, where duty is clearly defined; that of the dark, where wrong is no less clearly marked; and a great borderland of twilight, where there is no certainty, where dividing lines are not distinct, and where each man must be fully persuaded for himself. It is here, however, that the temper of the soul is tested. Here the decisions are come to that make us weak or strong. Here, that we may drift into the dark, or start a path of upward climbing that will conduct to the table-lands where the light never wanes. In threading a difficult way through these devious tracks, there is no clue so helpful or certain as to ask what will conduce to the praise of God. All that would hinder this must be avoided; all that would promote and enhance it must be followed at any cost.

We must also *shine*—and there is more in that expression than simply to do right—that men who see our good works may glorify our Father and give Him praise. It is through the Church that the principalities and powers

47

of heavenly places learn the manifold wisdom of God (Eph. 3:10).

We are disposed to dwell too exclusively on what God is to us—and indeed we can never make too much of the fact that the entire resources of his being, which the apostle Paul calls his fullness, are at our disposal. But let us not forget the other side of this great truth, and go on to know the riches of the glory of his inheritance in us his saints. Let us not forget so to yield Him every acre of our inner life, and every fragment of our time, that from these the great Husbandman may get for Himself crop after crop of praise; bringing all under cultivation, till the cornfields of the lowlands, the pomegranates of the orchards, the vineyards of the terraced heights, yield each in its measure their meed of adoration.

(2) THE POSSIBLE THWARTING OF HIS PURPOSE.—"Ye shall know the revoking of My promise" (Num. 14:34, R.V., marg.). There is nothing more terrible in the history of a soul than to frustrate the Divine ideal in its creation and redemption, and to prevent God deriving from us that for which He saved us. Such may be Thy lot, O figtree, standing straight in the pathway of the Son of Man, to which He comes, hungry for fruit: therefore, beware, and learn from this paragraph the symptoms of Israel's declension. Be warned by these, lest for thee also there come the suspension of the Divine purpose.

(1) *Prayerlessness.* "Thou has not called upon Me, O Jacob; but thou hast been weary of Me, O Israel" (verse 22). Nothing is a surer gauge of our spiritual state than our prayers. There may be a weariness of the brain which is the reaction of overstrain, and against which it is not wise to struggle. When mind and heart are so overpowered by the fatigues of the body that an inevitable drowsiness closes the eye and restrains the flow of thought, it is better to say with the great Bengel, as we yield ourselves to sleep, "O Lord, we are on the same terms as yesterday." But this is very different from the perfunctory and hurried devotions which arise from the preoccupation of the mind in things of time and sense, or the alienation of the heart from God by sin. If this lethargy is stealing over thee, beware!

(2) *Neglect of little things.* "Thou hast not brought Me the small cattle of Thy burnt-offerings" (verse 23). The emphasis is on the word *small*. The people were probably careful of the larger matters of Jewish ritual, but neglectful of the smaller details. None of us goes wrong at first in the breach of the great obligations of the law. It is the little rift in the lute, the tiny speck in the fruit, the small orifice in the bank, where deterioration begins. Nothing is really small that concerns God or the soul. Let us be careful about slight inaccuracies; small deviations from the strict integrity of a holy character; tampering with the gentler admonitions of conscience. Insensibility and carelessness in little things in a child are immediately corrected by the wise parent, who knows to what they may lead.

(3) *Lack of sweetness.* "Thou hast brought Me no sweet cane" (verse 24). It is possible to do right things from a hard sense of legalism, in which the sweetness and lovableness of true religion are painfully wanting. How often we do things because we must, or because we will, and not because we are led by the silken chains of love to our dear Lord! This is what the apostle calls being married to the law; instead of being united to the Man who was raised from the dead, and whose love should be the supreme constraint. His service is perfect freedom; his yoke is easy, and his burden is light.

Many are the instances of this change of purpose. David substituted for Saul; Solomon for Adonijah; the Church for the Hebrew people; Western for Eastern Christianity; the Moravians and Lollards for the established churches of their time. An instance was narrated recently of a church in the United States, which, by an immense majority, refused to receive coloured people into its communion. A few years after, it had so utterly declined that its building was for sale, and was purchased by the coloured congregation which had gathered around the members it had driven forth. So God takes away his kingdom from those that prove themselves unworthy of it, and gives it to such as will fulfil his purpose and set forth his praise. "Be not highminded, but fear; for if God spared not the natural branches, neither will He spare thee." (Rom. 11 : 20–21, R.V.).

(3) THE FULFILMENT OF GOD'S PURPOSE THROUGH OUR

PAIN.—"They *shall* show forth My praise" (verse 21). God's purpose cannot be ultimately set aside. It may be brought to a stand by some mountain of prejudice or unbelief; but it will be found pursuing its chosen path on the other side, having tunnelled, or climbed, or gone around it. So it shall be with Israel and with each of us. But the cost—how enormous!

In the case of mankind, God's purpose to give Adam and his race dominion over the works of His hands, was exposed to the terrific interruption of sin, which has cost four thousand years of untold anguish, besides the bloody sweat of Gethsemane, and the broken heart of Calvary. But, though suspended for four milleniums, the Divine thought in our creation shall yet take effect. The righteous shall have dominion in the morning. All enemies shall be put under our feet. The seed of the woman shall bruise the serpent's head. But, ah! the cost to God, to man, and to the travailing creation!

So in the case of Israel. She shall yet shine as a star, and sing God's praise like an angel chorister. But again the cost has been excessive. Sorrow such as this world has never seen has been the purifying furnace through which she has been purged from her dross, and poured into the mould, which from the first days of her history was waiting to give her the pre-destined shape.

So with each child in the family of God. The thoughts of his heart must stand; his ideal shall be realised; his purposes finally achieve their aim. This may be through the willing obedience and acquiescence of the soul; then there need be no great strain, or pressure, or anguish. Strength will be proportionate for every task; the back suited for every burden; the gradient adapted to the engine that has to climb its steep ascent. But if there is obstinacy, rebellion, murmuring complaint, like that which so often filled the camp of Israel, there will be suffering, exile; the wilderness with its desolation and monotony; the long waiting: and only after years of such discipline shall the soul come back again to stand at the gate of Canaan, and enter upon its inheritance, and give to the great Husbandman that praise and glory for which it was originally made.

Has this been thy history up till now? Then turn and repent. God declares that He will not remember the past with all its bitter disappointment and misappropriation of opportunity; that He will outdo the wonders of the bygone times by the mercies He will bestow; and that He will make a way through the wilderness, with flowing streams and waving verdure. What though thou hast brought thyself into the waste!—He will find a way forth into Canaan again. He will give thee thy vineyards from thence, and the valley of Achor for a door of hope; and thou shalt sing as in the days of thy youth. Formed for Himself, thou shalt yet show forth his praise. Yield to Him, that He may win from thee all on which He has set his heart, at once and easily. It shall be the best for thee.

8

A PERVERTED APPETITE

"All partial beauty was a pledge
Of beauty in its plenitude:
But since the pledge sufficed thy mood
Retain it! Plenitude be theirs
Who looked above!"

E. B. Browning

(Isaiah 44:20)

Two lessons were learnt by Israel in captivity—the all-sufficiency of God, and the absurdity of idols. Each of these themes is dealt with in the glowing sentences of the paragraph which commences at the sixth verse of this chapter and culminates with the twentieth verse.

The all-sufficiency of God is the subject of verses 6, 7, 8.

The absurdity of idols, verses 9 to 20.

It is on the latter of these that we are now to dwell. We are conducted into the idol-factories of the day. As we begin our exploration, we are forewarned that we shall find the manufacturers vain, and their delectable things unprofitable; and that the whole assembly of them stand together in solid phalanx, they shall be put to utter confusion and shame.

51

With this caution we enter the workshop where a molten image is being made from glowing metal, beneath the heavy blows of the hammer, wielded by the strong arm of the swarthy smith. Surely the product of such strength should be strong to help. But see, the smith himself is tired and thirsty after a few hours of work ; how evidently, then, is he unable to produce that which can help other men in the extremity of their need! The effect cannot be greater than its cause. An idol cannot give perennial strength, when its manufacturer is so easily exhausted (verse 12).

Next, we are led into a factory of wooden idols, where a carpenter is at work, stretching out a line of measurement, drawing a pattern with red ochre on the block of timber, and shaping the figure of a man. The floor is littered with crisp shavings, the furniture is heavy with sawdust, and the idol that is to fill its votaries with such awful dread is being very unceremoniously handled in its process of manufacture (verse 13).

Lastly, we follow some private individual into the forest. He levels cedar or oak ; or an ash tree, planted long before, because its durable wood, when grown, would well suit his purpose. Part of the tree is sawn into logs and stacked for firing, and the remainder is fashioned into an idol, before which he prostrates himself. How graphically are these contrasts portrayed. We can hear the chuckle of delight, as the man warms his hands or roasts his food by the crackling logs ; and immediately after we can see him in prayer, pleading with the remainder of the trunk to deliver him as his god.

Why do men act thus, with such inconceivable folly? How is it that they do not realise the incongruity of their actions? The prophet knows nothing of the modern theory that men do not worship the stone or wood, but accept the effigy as a help to fixedness of thought and prayer ; he would affirm that with the mass of men this is a fiction, and that the worship of the devotee stops short with what he can see and touch. The cause of idolatry lies deeper. "He feedeth on ashes ; a deceived heart hath turned him aside, that he cannot deliver his soul, nor say, Is there not a lie in my right hand?"

(1) THERE IS A HUNGER FOR THE DIVINE IN MAN.—*It is Universal*. All men are made on the same plan, whether

52

physically or morally. As the body needs food, so does the mind demand truth, and the spirit God. This is true of every age and clime. Always and everywhere these appetites demand satisfaction. Hence, beside the homes of men you will always find the corn-field, the mango-field, or the bread-fruit tree; and within a stone's throw a church, or chapel, or temple, the path to which is trodden hard by repeated steps.

It is significant. We can tell something of the composition of the human body by the materials which it needs for its sustenance. Similarly the true dignity of man betrays itself in the hunger which perpetually preys upon him. The cattle, when they have taken their full meal, repose contentedly on the grass; but man is not satisfied to have eaten his roast or warmed at his fire, he must needs go forth in search of the beautiful, the sublime, the harmony of sweet colours and sounds, the discovery of truth, the presence of God. Does not this disprove the materialistic philosophy in vogue in some quarters? If man is only matter, if thought is only the movement of the grey matter of the brain, if there is no spirit and no beyond, how is it that the material world cannot supply the supreme good? and that when, as in the case of Solomon, life is filled with all that wealth and power can yield, man turns from it all as a vain and empty bubble, the mirage of the desert, the apples of Sodom, the chaff which cannot appease hunger? Does not this show that there are component parts of man's nature, and these the noblest, which because they cannot be appeased by the contents of the time-sphere, are above time, and belong to the eternal and unseen? Must not there be something Divine in man, if he hungers for the Divine; something spiritual and eternal, since the spiritual and eternal alone can meet his need?

It is inevitable. The functions which food performs in our system are threefold. It is needed to replace the perpetual waste which is always wearing down the natural tissues; to maintain the temperature at some 98°; and to provide materials for growth. And each of these has a spiritual analogy. We need God for the same three reasons as the body needs food.

(1) We need God, to replace the perpetual waste of our spiritual forces. Each time we act or speak we expend

53

some portion of our nature; we break off, so to speak, some tiny fragment of nerve or muscle; we wear thinner some string or wheel in the complex physical machine. This needs to be renewed and replaced. Hence life is a perpetual struggle against the forces of disintegration and decay at work within us. Thus it is in the spiritual sphere also: each unselfish act; each remonstrance against wrong, or effort on the behalf of purity, peace, or righteousness; all right thinking, living, and working; all visits to the sick, discourses, acts of moral heroism, expend our spiritual forces. We are subject to a perpetual wearing down and consumption of spiritual energy. And therefore there must be hours of quiet fellowship with God, in which to recruit ourselves and regain our spent vigour.

(2) We need God for warmth and heat. In cold the body requires a good supply of carbon; it must be well fuelled. At every point of the immense system of blood-circulation there must be fires kept burning, to consume the waste products that choke the veins, and to maintain animal heat. So we need the comfort of the Comforter, the renewal of love and faith and hope, the blessed glow of those coals of juniper of which the Spouse speaks. And this, again, can only be met with in fellowship with God.

(3) We need God for growth. As the young child must have milk that it may grow thereby, and as the ravenous appetite of the growing lad or girl betrays the immense demand that nature is making for materials, out of which to build up her temple; so our spiritual growth depends on how much of God we can take into our being. For want of this Divine Food, some never get beyond the babe stage, to become strong men and women in Christ. That which builds up the inner life is deep and intimate fellowship with God; and the more direct it is the better.

(2) THIS APPETITE MAY BE PERVERTED.—"He feedeth on ashes." An appetite may be perfectly healthy in itself, but it may be supplied with unsuitable materials. In times of scarcity the Chinese use a kind of edible earth as a substitute for food. Negroes on the West Coast of Africa have been known to sustain life on a yellowish earth, used with coarse flour to make it go further; whilst the natives of Java are said to knead clay into balls for eat-

54

ing, as a luxury. In these ways men tamper with their natural appetite. They literally spend money for that which is not bread, and labour for that which satisfieth not.

But there is a close similarity in their treatment with that wonderful yearning after the unseen and eternal which is part of the very constitution of our being—a hunger after the ideal Food, the ideal Beauty, the ideal Truth, which may be resisted and ignored, but still claims satisfaction ; and if it does not get it in God, it will seek it in the ashes of idolatry.

Men worship idols yet. The sensualist worships in the old Temple of Venus, though he has never heard the murmur of the blue Ægean around the island dedicated to the grossest impurity under the name of religion. He tries to satisfy his hunger for Divine love with the ashes of physical gratification.

The man of the world worships money, rank, high office ; he is prepared to sacrifice everything to win them. Morning, noon, and night, he is expending his choicest gifts at the shrine of the god of this world, invoking his help, propitiating his wrath, endeavouring to win his smile. The golden calf is still the centre of worship, decorated by garlands. encircled by the merry crowds. Costly sacrifices smoke before it, though in the solemn heights of Sinai the cloud pavilion glows with the Shekinah.

The child of fashion worships in the temple of human opinion, and feeds on the ashes of human applause an appetite which was meant to satisfy itself on the "Well done!" of the Almighty.

The student who questions or denies the Being of God, worships in the temple of learning ; and feeds with the ashes of human opinion an appetite which was intended to be nourished by eternal truth.

The soldier, in whom the love of adventurous deeds is strong, is apt to worship in the Temple of Mars, and to feed with the ashes of military excitement an appetite which was intended to lead to great exploits on behalf of the oppressed and wronged. In one shape or another, idolatry is as rife among us as ever, though material emblems are in small request. And in every case these substitutes for God, with which men try to satisfy themselves, are as incapable of satisfying the heart, as ashes of supporting the physical life.

(3) THE TRUE BREAD.—*It is the Gift of God.* "My Father giveth the true bread from heaven." God who made thee hunger for Bread, made Bread to grow for its appeasement. There is, of course, the human side in the cultivation and preparation of food; but it is a small thing compared with the Divine. "Thou providest them corn, for so preparest Thou the earth" (Psa. 65, R.V., marg.). In every land there is the bread-stuff indigenous to the soil. Other vegetables have their peculiar habitat. The olive will not grow in Labrador, and the fir does not flourish on the banks of the Amazon. But the corn-plant will make its home in every land, and grow on every soil.

He has also provided Beauty for our taste, Truth for our thought, Love for our heart; and has gathered all these and much more into his one gift, Jesus Christ our Lord, who contains within himself all that is required for our inner life, as corn contains all that is needful for the nourishment of the body.

Nature yields her provision to man through death. The armies of standing corn are mowed down by the sickle. The tender plants yield up their stores, through the edge of steel, the grind of millstones, the scorch of fire, to minister to man. The cattle fall beneath the staggering blow, or the gash of the knife. For the wild things of the forest there are the rifle and swift death. So it is through death that Jesus has become the Food of men. The Lord's Supper perpetually reminds us of this. The bread and wine that nourish us there are the emblems of the flesh and the blood of One who has died and is risen again. At that holy feast we commemorate the death of One who lives for ever; and show forth that the life which nourishes our spirits has passed through the sharpness of death, that it might nourish within our spirits the eternal life. Our Lord's repeated reference to flesh and blood, which are so significant of death, enforces and accentuates this truth—that it is only through his death, and through our participation with Him of death, that He can become the true meat and the true drink (John 6:53–57).

Let it never be forgotten, that it is not by the words, nor example, nor deeds of Jesus Christ, alone and apart from his death, that we can grow into the stature of perfect men; but by fellowship with Him in death, and by the passage of all these qualities through death, and by

56

the careful pondering of his own words, "I was dead, and behold, I am alive for evermore." It is through death and resurrection that the Lord Jesus has become the food-stuff of the spiritual nature of man.

We must assimilate our food. It is not enough that the Lord Jesus should be set forth evidently crucified for us. We must feed on Him by faith. We must meditate on all that He is, and all that He has done. We must receive Him into our hearts by an act of spiritual apprehension. We must reckon that we have received and do possess. We must especially appropriate Him in respect of those special requirements which may have revealed themselves in moments of temptation and failure.

So shall we become strong and glad. Life in full measure will be meted out to us. We shall eat of the Tree of Life, which is in the midst of the Paradise of God. We shall know even as we are known.

9

THE GIRDINGS OF JEHOVAH

"Ere suns and moons could wax and wane,
  Ere stars were thunder girt, or piled
  The heavens, God thought on me His child,
Ordained a life for me, arranged
  Its circumstances every one
To the minutest; aye, God said,
  This head this hand shouldest rest upon
  Thus, ere He fashioned star or sun."

E. B. Browning

(Isaiah 45:5)

Cyrus, who is named here for the first time, is one of the noblest figures in ancient history. Herodotus and Xenophon are loud in his praise. A century after his death, as the latter travelled through Asia Minor, the impression of his noble personal character and wise

57

statesmanship was fresh and clearly defined. He must, indeed, have been a good and great man, whose character became a model for the Greek youth, in strength, simplicity, humanity, purity, and self-restraint. Such was God's chosen instrument for the great work of emancipating the chosen people and reinstating them in their own land.

We have seen that Jehovah assured the people graciously of their return from captivity at the end of the seventy years. Jerusalem should be built, and the cities of Judah inhabited (44:26). And they probably expected that the return would be signalised by miracles as stupendous as those which opened the door to freedom from the bondage of Egypt. Again the waters would start back, and the river divide; the floor of the desert would be strewn with manna, and rocks would gush with watersprings. But their deliverance was not to be on this wise. The miracle was to be wrought in the world of mind not of matter. By a series of unexpected providences, the Divine purpose was to be realised through a heathen monarch, who did not know Him by whom his strength was girded and his path prepared.

At the beginning of his career, Cyrus was chieftain of an obscure Persian tribe. His first success was in obtaining, whether by diplomacy or force, the leadership of two tribes of hardy mountaineers, at that time unknown beyond the narrow confines of their native hills. With these he began a course of conquest which swept from the frontier of India to the blue waters of the Ægean, subjugating even Crœsus, king of Lydia, whose wealth has passed into a proverb. Doors of opportunity opened before him quite marvellously; rough difficulties were levelled; hidden treasures fell into his hands, and the brazen doors stood open before his triumphant progress. All this time, though religious according to his light, and punctilious in acknowledging the gods of his people, he did not know Jehovah, by whom he was being girded and used.

At last, after years of unbroken victory, he stood knocking at the gates of Babylon, demanding from the son and grandson of Nebuchadnezzar the recognition of his supremacy. How little did he or they realise that this summons was the result of a Divine purpose, bent on securing the emancipation of the captive Jews, and their return to their sacred city, to become the religious leaders

58

of the world—the stock from which the true Servant and
Anointed of the Lord was to proceed!

For weary months Babylon withstood the siege, and
laughed to scorn the attempt of barbarous tribes to
scale her massive walls, or force her mighty gates. But one
night when, in fancied security, Belshazzar made a feast
to a thousand of his lords, and the vigilance of the
guards was relaxed, the mystic hand on the walls of the
royal banqueting-hall traced the decree that the kingdom was at an end, and had passed into the hands of the
Medes and Persians. That night Cyrus diverted the
mighty river that traversed the lordly city into a vast
reservoir, arranged for the storage of water ; and as it
left its ancient course, his troops marched along the
oozy channel, and burst into the city with loud cries
that startled the revellers at their cups, and the sleepers
in their dreams, inaugurating days of slaughter, rapine,
and pillage.

Daniel, venerable with age, was beyond controversy
the greatest subject of the realm. On the night of the
capture he had rebuked Belshazzar for his sins, and announced the conclusion of the siege. He held in his hand
the keys to the policy of the empire, and was therefore
at once sought after by Cyrus and his uncle Darius
(Dan. 6:2 ; 10:1). He had come to see that the period of
seventy years was now nearly ended (Dan. 9:2) ; and
he appears to have taken an early opportunity, at least so
Josephus says, of acquainting Cyrus with the history of
his people, and with those wonderful predictions that
had stood so long on the pages of their sacred books,
minutely predicting his career, and even his name. They
also gave forecast of what he was next to do. Notwith-
standing the predictions of Chaldean astrologers, God
had brought him to the throne of Babylon ; and, in spite
of all apparent unlikeliness, he would perform the counsel
of inspired messengers, saying of Jerusalem, "She shall
be inhabited ; and of the cities of Judah, they shall be
built" (Isa. 44:26). How startling it must have been, when
the aged prophet brought under the notice of the young
conqueror such words as these: "I have raised him up
in righteousness, and I will make straight all his ways:
he shall build my city, and he shall let go my captives,
not for price nor reward, saith the Lord of hosts" (45:13).

It is therefore not to be wondered at, that in the first

year of his reign he made a proclamation throughout all his kingdom, and put it also in writing, saying, "Thus saith Cyrus, king of Persia: All the kingdoms of the earth hath the Lord, the God of heaven, given me; and He hath charged me to build Him an house in Jerusalem, which is in Judah. Whosoever there is among you of all his people, his God be with him, and let him go up to Jerusalem, which is in Judah, and build the house of the Lord, the God of Israel" (Ezra 1:1–4, R.V.).

What a vast conception is here unfolded to us of the Providence that shapes man's ends, "rough-hew them as he will"! There is a plan which underlies the apparent chaos of worldly affairs, and is slowly achieving its ends; though the agents through which it is being executed are largely unaware of what is afoot. In the words of the greatest monarch of his time, whom Jehovah likened to a head of gold, and who had ample opportunity of verifying his conclusions, God does as He will among the inhabitants of the earth, and none can stay his hand or say, What doest Thou? (Dan. 4:35).

(1) GOD'S PLAN, AS IT AFFECTS SOCIETY.—(1) *It is comprehensive,* sweeping from age to age, threading milleniums, building its structure from the dust of earth's earliest age to the emergence of the new heavens and earth at the close of time.

But it is minute and particular. No great general can carry through a successful campaign who is not patient enough to attend to details. Wellington rode over to see Blucher the night before Waterloo, to know for himself when the Prussian legion would come through the forest of Soignies. God ordained the succession of William of Orange to the throne of England, in the place of the Stuarts; and it was his hand that made the wind veer from west to east at one critical moment in the night of his landing, or he had missed Torbay and been carried into the heart of the English fleet. Nothing is small with God. The sparrow does not fall to the ground without Him; and the tiniest events are woven into the scheme of his all-embracing providence. He makes even the sin and wrath of man to subserve his purpose.

(2) *He works through individuals.* The story of man is for the most part told in the biographies of men. It is

60

through human instruments that God executes his beneficent purposes, his righteous judgments. Through Columbus, He draws aside the veil from the coast line of
America. Through a Watt and a Stevenson, He endows
men with the co-operation of steam ; through a Galvani and
an Edison with the ministry of electricity. Through a De
Lesseps, He unites the waters of the eastern and western
seas, and brings the Orient and Occident together. Through
a Napoleon He shatters the temporal power of the Pope ;
and by a Wilberforce strikes the fetters from the slave.
Men do not know the purpose of God in what they are
doing. They arise and move onward in a course of unbroken success. They become accustomed to the opening
of barred gates, the unclosing of closed doors. They expect and win the highest positions, honours, and prizes
of the world. They credit themselves with what they
achieve ; and their fellows eagerly analyse their make-up
and methods to ascertain the secret of their great strength.
They know not that they are really instruments in the
Divine hand, surnamed and girded by One whom they
know not.

(3) *God's use of them does not interfere with their
free action.* This is clearly taught in more than one significant passage in Scripture. Joseph's brethren acted
on the promptings of their malicious hearts, and meant
only evil ; but God, all the while, was meaning and
achieving good to Joseph, to themselves, and to the land
of Egypt. Herod, Pilate, and the religious leaders of the
Jews, were swept before a cyclone of passion and jealousy ; and it was with wicked hands that they crucified
and slew the Lord of Glory: but they were accomplishing the determinate counsel of God, and doing whatsoever his hand and his counsel fore-ordained to come to
pass. We cannot understand this mystery, nor reconcile
the movements of the far-distant planets of this great
system. This arises from the limitation of our faculties
in this our nursery life. But we must accept it as true. It
is incontestably the teaching of Scripture, that a man
like Cyrus might be engaged in the pursuance of his own
schemes and ambitions, whilst, all the time, he was being
girded and used by One whom he did not know.
All these principles should be carefully conned and

prayerfully pondered. They underpin the life of society and of individuals also.

(2) GOD'S PLAN, AS IT AFFECTS INDIVIDUALS.—We are all concious of an element in life that we cannot account for. Other men have started life under better auspices, and with larger advantages than we, but somehow they have dropped behind in the race, and are nowhere to be seen. Our health has never been robust, but we have had more working days in our lives than those who were the athletes of our school. We have been in perpetual peril, travelling incessantly, and never involved in a single accident; whilst others were shattered in their first journey from their doorstep. Why have we escaped, where so many have fallen? Why have we climbed to positions of usefulness and influence, which so many more capable ones have missed? Why has our reputation been maintained, when better men than ourselves have lost their footing and fallen beyond recovery?

There is not one of us who cannot see points in the past where we had almost gone, and our footsteps had well-nigh slipped: precipices along the brink of which we went at nightfall, horrified in the morning to see how near our footprints had been to the edge. Repeatedly we have been within a hair-breadth of taking some fatal step, yielding to some impetuous temptation, striking a Faust-like bargain with the devil. How nearly we were caught in that eddy! How strangely we were plucked out of that companionship. How marvellously we were saved from that marriage, from that investment, from embraking in that ship, travelling by that train, taking shares in that company!

There is something to be explained in the lives of men which they cannot account for. They describe their consciousness of this anonymous element, as it has been called, by the words "luck," "fortune," "chance"; but these are mere subterfuges, sops thrown to silence the appeals of their common sense. We know better. It is God who has girded us, though we did not know Him.

It was God who opened those doors of opportunity; who smoothed those rough places, so that not a pebble remained at which to stumble; who gave treasures, where all had been dark; who unlocked gates of brass, which had threatened to bar the way. This is one of the luxuries of our mature years, to see all the way by which He has led us; it will be a cause of adoring gratitude as we review our life-course from the heights of heaven. As we stand there with God, He will show us how often our girdings to great tasks were due to his strong hands being placed around and upon us. He ever girds for tasks to which He calls. God cannot desert what has cost Him so much. He will finish what he has begun. He will lead thee o'er crag and torrent till the night is gone. He will not let one good thing fail. And, like the dying patriarch, standing on the verge of another world, thou wilt see the Angel who has redeemed thee from all evil.

When Peter stood with Jesus by the shores of the lake of Galilee He contrasted the independence of his earliest days, when he girded himself, and walked whither he would, with the dependence of those later days when he should stretch forth his hands, and another should gird and carry him. With these words our Lord signified the manner of death in which he should glorify God. What was true of the helplessness of Peter's old age and martyrdom, should be true of each of us in the intention and choice of the soul. Let us give up girding ourselves in the assertion of our own strength, and stretch forth our hands, asking our Lord to gird us and carry us whither He will, even to death, if thereby we may the better glorify God.

10

ASKING AND COMMANDING

"Say what is Prayer, when it is Prayer indeed?
The mighty utterance of a mighty need.
The man is praying, who doth press with might
Out of his darkness into God's own light."

Trench

(Isaiah 45:2)

An exquisite image stands like an initial letter at the beginning of the paragraph of which these words form part. To the eye of the seer the earth lies open to heaven as a wide corn-land over which the clouds of heaven hang, the air breathes, and the sun sheds sheets of light. Those clouds are big with righteousness, the special term used throughout this book of the faithfulness of Jehovah. At the call of prayer the skies pour down their precious treasure, and the earth opens every pore to receive the plentiful rain; presently, every acre brings forth salvation, and righteousness springs up in the hearts of men, as their answer to the descent of the righteousness of God. It is the bridal of heaven and earth, a fulfilment of the prediction of the psalm—"Truth springeth out of the earth; and righteousness hath looked down from heaven."

The conception is one of surpassing beauty. The brooding of heaven; the response of earth. Deep calling unto deep. The nature of God originating and inspiring; the nature of man responding. And when the descending grace of God is thus received by the believing, yearning heart of man the result is *salvation*. As the margin of R.V. reads: "Let the skies be fruitful in salvation, and let the earth cause righteousness to spring up together." The whole paragraph to the close of the chapter rings with *salvation* as its keynote. Does God hide Himself? He is the God of Israel, the Saviour. Are the makers of idols ashamed and confounded? Yet Israel is saved with an everlasting salvation. Are graven images held up to contempt? It is because they are gods that cannot save. Does God assert his unrivalled Deity? It is because He is a just God, and a Saviour. Are men bidden to look to Him, though they be far removed as the ends of the earth? It is that they may be saved.

Primarily, no doubt, this salvation concerns the emancipation of the chosen people from the thraldom of Babylon, and their restoration to Jerusalem. "He shall build my city; he shall let my exiles go free, not for price nor reward, saith the Lord of Hosts." This deliverance, which is a type of the greater deliverance from the guilt and power of sin, was, in the fixed purpose of God, sure as the creation of the earth and man; guaranteed by the hands that stretched out the heavens, and by the word that commanded all their host. As certainly as God was God, He would bring His people again to the land which He gave to their fathers to inherit.

But now, side by side with this avowal of the Divine determination, this strange command breaks in, the importance of which is accentuated by the threefold description of the speaker. "THE LORD"—that is, God in his everlasting redemptive purpose; "the Holy One of Israel" —that is, the moral perfections of Israel's God, as contrasted with the abominations perpetrated with the sanction of heathen religions; "his Maker"—suggesting the purpose which from the clay, gathered in Abraham's time from the highlands of Mesopotamia, was fashioning a fair vessel meet for His use. This threefold description of God introduces the august command which bade the people seek by prayer the fulfilment of the purpose on which the Divine heart was set.

In launching an ironclad, the pressure of a baby's finger is not infrequently required to put in operation the ponderous machinery by which the iron leviathan glides evenly and majestically on to the ocean wave. So, if we may dare to say it, all the purposes of God, and the providential machinery by which they were to be executed, stood in suspense until the chosen people had asked for the things which He had promised, and had even commanded Him concerning the work on which his heart was set. The victorious career of Cyrus; the dissatisfaction of the priestly caste with the king of Babylon; the evident signs of the disruption of the mighty empire; the near completion of the seventy years, foretold by Jeremiah—all were in vain, unless, like Daniel, the people set their face unto the Lord God, to seek the fulfilment of his word, by prayer and supplications, with fasting, and sackcloth, and ashes (Dan. 9:3).

(1) PRAYER IS A NECESSARY LINK IN THE PERFORMANCE OF THE DIVINE PROMISES.—"Ask Me of things to come." God is always saying, "Ask, seek, knock." Even to the Son, Jehovah says, "Ask of Me, and I will give Thee the nations for Thine inheritance, and the uttermost parts of the earth for Thy possession." And to the chosen people, at the end of a paragraph jewelled with "I wills," and unfolding the work which He is prepared to do—not for their sakes, but for his own—He says, "For this, moreover, will I be inquired of by the house of Israel, to do it for them." Our Lord is unremitting in the stress He lays on prayer, and pledges Himself to do only whatsoever is asked in his name. The apostle James insists

that one reason why we have not, is that we ask not (Psa. 2:8; Ezek. 36:37; John 14:13; James 4:2).

The declaration of our text is therefore supported by a wealth of Scripture testimony for the necessity of prayer, as a link in the accomplishment of the Divine purpose.

(1) Prayer is part of the system of co-operation between God and man, which pervades nature and life. No crop waves over the autumn field, no loaf stands on our breakfast table, no metal performs its useful service, no jewel sparkles on the brow of beauty, no coal burns in hearth or furnace—which does not witness to this dual workmanship of God and man. So in the spiritual world, there must be co-operation, though on the part of man it is often limited to prayers, which may seem faint and feeble, but which touch the secret springs of Deity; as the last pick of the miner may break open a fountain of oil, or a cavern set with dazzling jewels.

(2) Prayer, when genuine, indicates the presence of a disposition to which God can entrust his best gifts without injury to the recipient. To bless some men, apart from humility, and submission, and weanedness of soul from creature aid, would only injure. And so, in his dear love, God withholds his choicest gifts until the heart is sore broken, and cries to Him. That cry is the blessed symptom of soul-health. Like the sneeze of the child on which the prophet stretched himself, it indicates returning life; and such a temper of heart as may receive, without danger, blessings whose height was never reached by the majestic flight of eagle, and whose depths are beyond the fathoming line of the profoundest thought.

(3) Prayer is also in its essence, when inspired by faith, an openness towards God, a receptiveness, a faculty of apprehending with open hand what He would impart. Standing upon His promises, the suppliant cries to the heavens to drop down their blessings; whilst heart, and hands, and mouth are open wide to be filled with good. Therefore, let us pray.

Let us pray *unitedly*. God loves the gates of Zion where the throngs gather, more than the dwellings of Jacob where single families join in prayer. He would be inquired of by the *house* of Israel. If, when a petition is being prepared by a community to the sovereign, only two or three put their hands to it, it is set aside as undeserving

66

of attention. And what does God think of the earnestness of his people for the realisation of his promises
when only two or three gather in the place of prayer?

Let us pray *sympathetically*. The gathering for prayer
must not be of bodies only but of souls. When one prays
audibly, all should pray silently. A prayer offered in
the presence of others should receive their endorsement.
Soliloquy, disputation, enforcement of some special view
of truth, are out of place in the offerer of prayer ; whilst
listlessness, wandering thought, and the mere attitude
of attention, are out of place in those who, with bowed
forms and covered faces, assume the posture of devotion.

Let us pray *earnestly*. Prayer is measured, not by length,
but by strength. The Divine gauge of the worth of prayer
is its pressure on the heart of God. The lock of prayer
sometimes goes hard, and calls for strength of purpose.
The Kingdom of Heaven has to be taken by force. There
is such a thing as labouring and striving in prayer. Thus
Jesus prayed in the garden ; and Daniel in Babylon ; and
Epaphras in Paul's hired house. Such were the prayers
offered of old in the catacombs as the torchlight flick-
ered ; in Alpine caves where Waldenses cowered ; on hill-
sides where the Covenanters sheltered under the cliffs.
Let us pray so that our prayers may reverberate with repeated blows on the gates of God's presence-chamber,
"Praying always with all prayer and supplication, and
watching thereunto with all perseverance and supplication
for all saints." Let us pray, remembering that everything
depends on the gracious promise of God, but as if the
answer depended on the strength and tenacity of our
entreaty.

Let us pray *in the name of Jesus*. It is possible to be
so absorbed in the cause of our Lord, to be so eaten up
with the zeal of his house, so one with Him, that his interests and ours become identical. Then, when we pray, it
is almost as though the Son were addressing the Father
through our lips, and pouring forth a stream of intercession and petition by us. This is what He meant when He
repeatedly insisted on our praying in his name. The filial
spirit, that looks into the face of God, and says "Father" ;
the unselfish spirit, which is quite prepared to renounce
all if only God is exalted ; the loving spirit, which has its
centre in the interests of its Lord—all this is compre-
hended in the prayer we offer in the name of Jesus. And

when we pray thus, we secure the accomplishment of the things to come which God has promised.

(2) THE IMPERATIVE ACCENT IN FAITH.—"Concerning my sons, and concerning the work of my hands, command ye Me." Our Lord spoke in this tone when He said, "Father, I will." Joshua used it, when in the supreme moment of triumph, he lifted up his spear towards the setting sun, and cried, "Sun, stand thou still!" Elijah used it, when he shut the heaven for three years and six months, and again opened it. Luther used it, when, kneeling by the dying Melanchthon, he forbade death to take his prey.

It is a marvellous relationship into which God bids us enter. We are accustomed to obey Him. We are familiar with words like those which follow in this paragraph: "I, even My hands have stretched out the heavens, and all their host have I commanded." But that God should invite us to command Him! This is a change in relationship which is altogether startling. But there is no doubt as to the literal force of these words. With the single limitation that our biddings must concern his sons, and the work of his hands, and must be included in his word of promise, Jehovah says to us, his redeemed children in Jesus Christ, "Command ye Me!"

What a difference there is between this attitude and the hesitating, halting, unbelieving prayers to which we are accustomed, and which by their perpetual repetition lose edge and point! We do not expect that God will answer them now and here; but some day, on the far horizon of time, we imagine that they may achieve something, as waters, by continual lapping, wear a channel through the rocks.

How often during his earthly life did Jesus put men into a position to command Him! When entering Jericho, He stood still, and said to the blind beggars, "What will ye that I should do unto you?" It was as though He said, I am yours to command. And can we ever forget how he yielded to the Syro-phœnician woman the key to his resources, and told her to help herself even as she would? Long familiarity with Him even affected the speech of the apostles; for in their Spirit-inspired prayers we can detect this same tone of command, "And now, Lord, look upon their threatenings ; and grant unto Thy servants to speak Thy word with all boldness."

What mortal mind can realise the full magnificence of the position to which our God lovingly raises his little children? He seems to set them beside Himself on his throne, and says, while the fire of his Spirit is searching and ridding them of sordid and selfish desire, "All my resources are at your command, to accomplish anything which you have set your hearts upon. Whatsoever ye shall ask, that will I do."

The world is full of mighty forces which are labouring for our weal. Light, that draws our pictures for us ; magnetism, that carries our messages ; heat, that labours in our locomotives and foundries ; nitrogen, that blasts the rocks—these and many more. So much is this the age of machinery and contrivance, that the physical faculties of civilized races are deteriorating through disuse. Man is becoming increasingly proficient in the art of controlling the mighty forces of the universe, and yoking them to the triumphal car of his progress. Thus his old supremacy over the world is being in a measure restored to him.

How is it that these great natural forces—which are manifestations of the power of God—so absolutely obey man? Is it not because, since the days of Bacon, man has so diligently studied, and so absolutely obeyed, the conditions under which they work? "Obey the law of force, and the force will obey you," is almost an axiom in physics. If you will study, for instance, the laws of electricity, and carefully obey them, laying down the level track along which its energy may proceed, you can lead the stream whither you choose, and make it do whatever you appoint. All that is required from you is exact compliance with the requirements of its nature. So God gives the Holy Spirit to them that obey Him.

All the resources of God dwell bodily in the risen and glorified Lord. They are imparted to us through the communion of the Holy Spirit, who goes between the unsearchable riches of Christ and our poverty ; bringing the one to the other, as the ocean brings the wealth of the world up to the wharves of London or New York. We have then to deal with the Holy Spirit, to study the methods of his operation—what hinders or helps, what accelerates or retards. Obey Him, and He pours such

69

mighty energy into and through the spirit, that men are amazed at the prodigality of its supply; resist or thwart Him, and He retires from the spirit, leaving it to struggle as best it may with its difficulties and trials.

Yield thyself to God, O soul of man! Whatsoever He saith unto thee, do it. Be careful, even to punctiliousness, in thine obedience. Let God have his way with thee. In proportion as thou wilt yield to God, thou shalt have power with God. The more absolutely thou art a man under authority to the Commander-in-Chief, the more thou shalt be able to say to this and the other of his resources, Go, or Come, or Do this. God will be able to trust thee and give thee his key, bidding thee help thyself. Thou wilt be admitted to terms of such intimacy with God, that thou shalt hear Him bidding thee command Him. And, whilst never forgetting the reverence that becomes a subject, and the attitude that befits a saved sinner, thou shalt speak with Him concerning his sons and concerning the work of his hands.

But after our greatest deeds of prayer and faith, we shall ever lie low before God; as Elijah did, who, after calling fire from heaven, prostrated himself on the ground, with his face between his knees. The mightiest angels of God's presence-chamber bend the lowest; the holiest souls present perpetually the sacrifice of the broken and contrite spirit; the power to move the arm that moves the world is wielded by those who can most humbly adopt the confession, "I am a worm, and no man."

11

GOD OUR BURDEN BEARER

"Faint not! There is who rules the storm—Whose hand
Feeds the young ravens, nor permits blind chance
To close one sparrow, flagging wing in death.
Trust in the Rock of Ages. Now, even now
He speaks and all is calm."

Gisborne

(Isaiah 46:4)

This is an incident in the Fall of Babylon. Cyrus has broken in, and the mighty city lies open to the Persian army, exasperated by long waiting at her gates. The blood of her nobles has flowed freely over the marble floors of her palaces ; most of her defenders are slain. Women and children are cowering in the inmost recesses of their homes, or filling the streets with screams of terror and appeals for help, as they fly from the brutal soldiery. The final and most sanguinary conflicts have taken place within the precincts of the idol temples ; but all is still now. The priests have fallen around the altars which they served ; their blood mingling with that of their victims, and their splendid vestments are become their winding sheets. And now, down the marble staircases, trodden in happier days by the feet of myriads of votaries, lo, the soldiers are carrying the helpless idols. The stern monotheism of Persia would have no pity for the many gods of Babylon ; there are no idolshrines in the land of the sun-worshippers where they could find a niche: but they are borne away as trophies of the completeness of the victory.

There is Bel, whose name suggested that of the capital itself! How ignominiously it is handed down from its pedestal! And Nebo follows. The hideous images lavishly inset with jewels, and richly caparisoned, are borne down the stately steps, their bearers laughing and jeering as they come. The gods get little respect from their rude hands, which are only eager to despoil them of a jewel. And now at the foot of the stairs they are loaded up on the backs of elephants, or pitched into the ox-wagons. In more prosperous days they were carried with excessive pomp through the streets of Babylon, wherever there was plague or sickness. Then the air had been full of the clang of cymbals and trumpets, and the streets thronged with worshipping crowds; but all that is altered. "The things that ye carried about are made a load, a burden to the weary beast. They stoop, they bow down together; they could not deliver the burden, but themselves are gone into captivity" (46:1, 2, R.V.). So much for the gods of Babylon being borne off into captivity.

Close on this graphic picture of the discomfiture of the gods of Babylon, we are invited to consider a description of Jehovah, in which the opposite to each of these items stands out in clear relief. He speaks to the house of Jacob, and to all the remnant of the house of Israel, as children whom He had borne from the birth, and carried from earliest childhood. Their God needed not to be borne, He bore; needed no carriage, since his everlasting arms made cradle and carriage both. Such as He had been, He would be. He would not change. He would carry them, even to hoary hairs. He had made and He would bear; yea, He would carry, and deliver.

This contrast is a perpetual one. Some people carry their religion; other people are carried by it. Some are burdened by the prescribed creeds, ritual, observances, exactions, to which they believe themselves to be committed. Others have neither thought nor care for these things. They have yielded themselves to God, and are persuaded that He will bear them and carry them, as a man doth bear his son, in all the way that they go, until they come to the place of which God has spoken to them (Deut. 1:31; Isa. 63:9).

(1) THE BURDENS FOR WHICH GOD MAKES HIMSELF RESPONSIBLE.—The lives of most of us are heavily weighted. We began our race unencumbered, but the years as they have passed have added burdens and responsibilities. We run heavily; we walk with difficulty; we carry weights as well as sins.

Foremost there is the burden of existence. We must live. We were not asked if we would live; we are. We had no option than to live, and we have none to-day. The physical phenomenon, which men call death, may insert a comma, or draw a line ; but life continues yonder if not here, somehow if not thus, and for ever. Just because the spark on our heart-altars has been kindled at the eternal fires of the Divine nature, it will exist when the moon is withered with age, and the stars have burnt out in night.

There is the burden of sin. The word used of bearing is the same as Isaiah uses of the Sin-bearer, who bore our sins in his own body on the tree (53 : 4). Though the atmosphere presses upon us at the rate of several pounds for every square inch of bodily surface, we are yet unconscious of its weight. So, till Jesus came, man hardly realised the burden of sin, and groaned not beneath its intolerable weight. But as his pure image has passed from land to land, from age to age, it has convinced men of the awful burden of sin. This is shown to be the reason why they are weary and heavy-laden ; why their spirits lack joy and elasticity ; why the step tires so soon ; and the day of life drags so wearily to a close. And as the reason is given, we know it is so, and assent to Peter's cry, "I am a sinful man, O Lord."

There is the burden of responsibility for others. Our life is so closely entwined with that of others, that we cannot live long without becoming weighted with care for them. The son must care for mother and sisters. The young man is linked in imperishable bonds to the twin-soul, which is dearer than himself, and whose sorrows and anxieties mean more than his own. Then the sweet children who come into our lives, with their guileless trust ; the charge of others bequeathed with dying breath ; the care of employee, lonely ones, tempted and persecuted ones. Ah, it is impossible for thee or me to move so quickly as we did years ago!

There is also the burden of our life-work. That we have been sent to do what no one else can do ; that we have talents intrusted of which we must give an account ; that we are called to cultivate one patch in the vineyard ; to build one bit in the wall ; to utilise one talent of the Master's capital—this makes us sensible of the importance and urgency of life. It is not possible to realise what our life may mean of blessing or sorrow to others, and not feel the solemn weight of responsibility impinging on us.

In all these things we are doomed to be solitary. It cannot be otherwise. Each man and woman in our circle is similarly weighted. All have as much hill-climbing, burden-bearing, and fighting, as they can manage. None can share aught of his oil, or strength, or courage. We can give sympathy, but that is all. Each human soul must bear his own burden of existence, sin, responsibility, and work. But it is just here that Jehovah steps in. He does not distinguish between our burdens and ourselves ; but takes us and them up in his almighty arms, and bears us with no sense of fatigue, no fear of failure. We are a dead-weight ; but it matters nought to Him. He has borne us all the days of old: He daily beareth our burdens. He will bear us and carry us till He sets us down in the land where no burdens can enter ; the city through whose gates they are never borne ; the world, where the heavy-laden leap as an hart, and the weary are at rest.

(2) THE REASON WHY GOD ASSUMES THIS RESPONSIBILITY. —"I have made, and I will bear." When a parent sees his own evil nature re-appearing in his child—the same temper, the same passions, the same peculiarities—so far from casting that child aside, and quoting its faults as reasons for disowning it, he draws nearer to it, filled with a great pity, and murmurs, "I have made, and I will bear."

When a man has elicited in another a love which will never be at rest till it has nestled to his heart, even though considerations arise which make it questionable whether he has been wise, yet, as he considers the greatness of the love which he has evoked, he says to himself, "I have made, and I will bear."

When a Christian minister has gathered around him a large congregation, and many have been converted from the world, as he looks around on those who count him captain or father, he says to himself, when voices summon him elsewhere, unless some over-mastering consideration is pressed upon him, "I have made, and I will bear."

Now let us ascend by the help of these reflections, to the Divine nature, which is not above similar consider-ations. He has made and fashioned us ; He has implanted within us appetites that only He can satisfy ; He has

74

placed us amid circumstances of unusual difficulty, and intrusted to us work of unwonted importance; He has committed to us the post of duty which taxes us to the uttermost: and because He has done all this, He is responsible for all that is needed for the accomplishment of his purposes. Since all things are of Him, we may rest assured that they will be through Him and to Him for ever. He has made, and He will bear. He has incurred the responsibility of making us what we are, and placing us where we are; then He must perfect that which concerneth us, since his mercy endureth for ever—and He cannot forsake the work of his own hands.

There are several corroborations of this thought in the Bible. There is that word of our Lord, in which He tells us that our heavenly Father is bound to give meat for the hunger, and clothes for the body which He has given. There is the statement that what God has wrought us for, and given the earnest of, He must complete. There is the golden chain of Rom. 8, each link in which postulates the next, and that the next; predestination involves calling, and this justification, and this again glory. When God thinks of building a character He first considers whether He can complete it; and if He begin, it is a positive assurance that He will carry out his plan. What He makes, He will bear.

It was so with Israel. He made the chosen people by his election and grace. From an obscure tribe of Bedawin, He made them his peculiar people, his own inheritance, his messengers to the world. Notwithstanding their many wanderings and provocations, He has never put away the people whom He foreknew; through all these weary centuries He has been deeply solicitous for them, and He will yet bring them on eagles' wings to their city and land.

It is so with our world. He made it. It was the nurseling of his love and power, and bore the early imprint of his benediction. Through the depths of space He has never ceased to bear it, although it has been dark with sin and red with crime. He bore its contumely and shame when they cast Him forth with contempt to the cross. He bore its sin in the agony of Calvary. And the end is sure. He bears it on his heart, and will never put it away until its evil is overcome with his good, and it shines again in its early beauty and sings in unison with its sister spheres.

(3) THE CONSOLATION WHICH ARISES FROM THESE CONSIDERATIONS.

In hours of anguish for recent sin. The sin is our own. In no sense can the sinner lay it on God. "I have sinned," he cries, "and perverted that which was right, and it did not profit me. The sin is mine." And yet from the depth of sin-consciousness there is an appeal to God. He created, permitted us to be born as members of a sinful race. He knew all we should be, before He set his heart upon us and made us his own. May we not ask Him to bear with us whom He made, redeemed, and took to be his children by adoption and grace? And will He not answer, "I have made, and I will bear"?

In moments of great anxiety. When burdened with care for ourselves or others, we fall at the foot of the altar-steps that slope through darkness to God ; when our circumstances are beyond measure perplexing, and the knots refuse to be untied ; when we have no idea what to do, or how to act for the best—is there not every reason to look into the face of God, and say, "Thou hast permitted me to come hither, Thou alone knowest what I should do, Thou hast made me ; wilt Thou not bear me through this swelling tide and bring me on to firm standing-ground?" And will He not again answer, "I have made, and I will bear."?

In days of anxious foreboding. Sometimes, as we have climbed to an Alpine summit, the gaunt black rocks have risen around us from an ocean-surface of fleecy clouds, which have, so to speak, washed up against them, filling the whole intermediate valley. The hamlet where we were to spend the night, and the road to it, were alike hidden. So the future is hidden from our view, and with the fear born of ignorance we dread what may be awaiting us. The veil is slight, but impenetrable. What may it not conceal? Then again, we turn to the ineffable God. He knows all that we can bear, for He made us. It is not likely that He will imperil that on which He has spent time and thought. He cannot fail or forsake. We may freely cast on Him the responsibility.

O our Maker! bear us, as a mother her infant ; as a father his tired boy ; as a guide the fainting woman turned dizzy at the vision of sheer depth beneath: Thou hast made, wilt Thou not bear? Again the answer returns, "Even to old age I am He, and to hoary hairs will I carry you ; I have made, and I will bear, I will carry and will deliver."

12

SUMMONED TO AN EXODUS

"Think not of rest, though dreams be sweet;
Start up, and ply your heavenward feet!
Is not God's oath upon your head,
Ne'er to sink back on slothful bed;
Never again your loins untie
Nor let your torches waste and die?"

Keble

(Isaiah 48 : 20)

We now reach the close of the first part of these wonderful prophecies. It really concludes at the end of the forty-eighth chapter, with the summons to the house of Jacob, called by the name of Israel, which had come forth from the waters of Judah, to arise and go forth from Babylon.

There has never been an era in which God's people have not been face to face with a great principle of evil, embodied in a city, confederation, or conspiracy of darkness. Always the same spirit under differing forms ; always the deification of the human against the Divine ; always the pride and vainglory of intellect against moral worth ; always the effort of man's prowess and scheming to build a fabric without the Divine keystone which alone can give solidity and permanence.

This great system is as strong to-day as when the massive walls of Babylon enclosed their millions, and proudly dominated the world. Some have identified it with the Church of Rome, or the spirit of ecclesiastical assumption; but it is better to consider it as that element which is ever working through human society, which is spoken of as "the world," and of which the apostle said, "It is without hope and without God." We are therefore warranted in applying to present surroundings every item in the description given of the olden foe of Israel, and of heeding the summons to go forth.

(1) SENT TO BABYLON.—God's ideal for the chosen people is set forth under a beautiful similitude (18).

Their peace might have been as a river. Not as the brook, as it gushes rapturously forth, breaking musically on the stones, and flashing in the glee of its early life; not as a streamlet hardly filling its wide bed, and scarcely affording water enough for the fish to pass to its higher reaches; but like a river far down its course, sweeping along with majestic current, deep and placid, able to bear navies on its broad expanse, to collect and carry with it the refuse of towns upon its banks without contamination, and approaching the sea with the sympathy begotten of similarity in depth and volume and service to mankind. Oh, rivers that minister perpetually to man—not swept by storm, nor drained by drought, not anxious about continuance, always mirroring the blue of the azure sky, or the stars of night, and yet content to stay for every daisy that sends its tiny root for nourishment—in your growth from less to more, your perennial fullness, your beneficent ministry, your volume, your calm, ye were meant to preach to man, with perpetual melody, of the infinite peace that was to rise and grow, and unfold with every stage of his experience! Such at least was God's ideal for Israel, and for all who swear by his name and make mention of Jehovah as God.

Their righteousness might have been as the waves of the sea. Walk along the coast-line when the tide has ebbed, mark the wastes of sand, the muddy ooze, the black unsightly rocks. Not thus did God intend that any of his children should be. It was never his will that their righteousness should ebb, that there should be wastes, and gaps, and breaks in their experience, that there should be the fatal lack of strength, and purity and virtue. The Divine ideal of the inner life is mid-ocean, where the waves reach to the horizon on every side, and there are miles of sea-water beneath. No one can look upon the majestic roll of the Atlantic breakers, in purple glory, crowned with the white crest of foam, chasing one another as in a leviathan game, without realising the magnificence of the Divine intention that all who have learnt to call God Father, should be possessed of a moral nature as fresh, as multitudinous, as free in its motion, as pure in its character, as those waves which, far out to sea, lift up their voice and proclaim the wealth of the power of God.

What a contrast this to the troubled sea to which the wicked are compared—sighing, chafing, moaning along the shore, and casting up mire and dirt. Give me a thousand times rather mid-ocean, where the breezes blow fresh over miles of sea, than the melancholy break of the waves on a low and sandy shore. The one is as the righteous man in the strength and glory of his regenerate and justified manhood ; the other as the wicked, always churning, fretting, bringing forth that which will profit him nothing.

This ideal is within the reach of every one who will hearken to God's commandments. There is a short and easy method by which that peace may begin to flow for thee and me, and the waves of that righteousness sweep in jubilant measure over our souls. Hearken and do. Have his commandments and keep them. Level your life to your light. But if we refuse, and turn aside and follow the devices and desires of our evil hearts, we shall miss inevitably and utterly the realisation of that purpose which otherwise would make music in our hearts and melody to our God. Obedience to the least wish of the Lord, however and wherever expressed, is the golden secret, by the practice of which we may attain to this peace and this righteousness.

But if we refuse, we may have to pass, as Israel did, into the furnace of suffering in the Babylon of the world. God cannot be thwarted in the realisation of his purpose. If we are obstinate, and our neck an iron sinew, and our brow brass (4) ; if we trust in our idol and graven image (5) ; if we will not hear, nor know, nor open our ear (8)—then we must go by a more circuitous and painful route, via Babylon, with its bitter anguish, where, as in a furnace for silver, the dross and alloy will be purged away. How many of God's people are at this moment

79

in the furnace, which would not have been required if they had been willing and obedient! Not that the furnace always indicates unfaithfulness; but if we are unfaithful, we must expect the furnace.

(2) LIFE IN BABYLON.—The mighty city was called the Lady of Kingdoms. We must think of her with massive walls, broad spaces, colossal bulls guarding the entrances to vast temples with flights of stairs and terraces; with pyramids, towers, and hanging-gardens; her wharves receiving the freights of the Indian Ocean; her marts thronged with the merchants of the world; her streets teeming with tributary populations. But right across her splendour ran the fatal bars of cruelty, luxury, wickedness, and devil-worship.

Cruelty. When God gave his people into her hand, she showed them no mercy; but laid her yoke very heavily upon the aged, who staggered beneath their loads, or fainted in the horrors of the march to Babylon, whilst multitudes of the young were crucified among the smoking remnants of their city (47:7).

Luxury. She was given to pleasures, and dealt very carelessly. Her citizens were arrayed in fine linen and purple and scarlet, and decked with gold, precious stones, and pearls. Her merchandise was of gold, silver, precious stones, pearls, fine linen, purple, silk, and scarlet, ivory and brass, cinnamon and spice (8).

Wickedness. In this she trusted: in violence and oppression, in drunkenness and excess, in the impurities of nature-worship; so that she made all the nations drunk with the wine of her abominations (10).

Devil-worship. She laboured with her enchantments and with the multitudes of her sorceries (12).

Amid such scenes the Jews spent the weary years of their captivity. Very bitter was their lot. They were for a prey or a spoil. Bills of slave-sales which have been recently deciphered contain Jew-names. The majority of them were probably employed in exacting toils, in building up the material strength and prosperity of Babylon, as their fathers had done for Egypt centuries before.

But through this awful discipline there was slowly emerging a nobler, loftier ideal, which was fostered by the ancient words that foretold their destiny. It was not possible that they should be long holden by their captors. Were they not the elect people of God, destined to bless the world? Were they not called to bear the Ark of God in the march of the race? Was not the Covenant, made of old with Abraham, still vital in all its provisions? Yes, they might be in Babylon like many another captive people, but they had a great hope at their heart. And in the light of that hope, under the searching fires of their anguish, they for ever abandoned their love for idolatry; they turned from the outward rites of worship, to cultivate a strong moral and religious life; and they gave themselves up to the study of their inspired Scriptures with an ardour which, from that moment, made the synagogue and the scribe an indispensable adjunct of their national life. Never again was the Jew an idolater. Always after conscience was quick and sensitive. Without exception, the Jewish Scriptures, kept with the most exact and scrupulous care, and the Jewish synagogue, accompanied the movements of the scattered race. In addition, there was a breadth of view, enlarged conceptions of the dealings of God with man, an expansion of interests, which prepared the way for the further revelations of the Gospel as to the catholicity of the love of God, and the brotherhood of man. As a river, in its flow over various soils, becomes impregnated with their products, so did the Jewish people receive lasting benefits from their painful sojourn in Babylon, with whose waters they so often mingled their tears.

Some who read these words now are in their Babylon. They look back to a sunny past, which might have continued had they not stepped out of the narrow path of obedience. Their peace was then as a river, their righteousness as the waves of the sea; but, alas! all this is but a memory. They involved themselves in coils of difficulty and suffering, from which deliverance appears hopeless. The weary years seem destined to run out their slow and painful course without remedy. Yet let such still hope in God; they shall still praise Him; let them repent of their sins and put them away; let them learn the deep lessons which God's Spirit is endeavouring to teach; let them dare to praise God for the discipline of pain. In these dark hours light is being sown for the righteous, and gladness for the upright in heart. Presently the clarion call of the Exodus will ring out: "Arise and depart, for this is not your rest; cry unto her, that her warfare is accomplished, that her iniquity is pardoned; go ye forth of Babylon, flee ye from the Chaldeans."

(3) EXODUS FROM BABYLON.—The old order was changing and giving place to the new. In a magnificent apostrophe, the virgin daughter of Babylon had been summoned to come down from her imperial throne and sit on the ground. She was no more to be called tender and delicate. She must step down to the level of the common household drudge, who grinds the meal and carries the burden of the house. Loss of children and widowhood were to come to her in a moment—in one day; and neither the enchantments of magicians, nor the efforts of those who had traded with her, would avail to avert her calamities (47:1, etc.).

From the ruins of the mightiest city that, perhaps, the world has ever seen the Jews are bidden to go forth. "Go ye forth of Babylon, flee ye from the Chaldeans." The edict of Cyrus was only the countersigning of the Divine edict, which had already gone forth. And it is very remarkable that whilst Babylon has vanished, leaving no trace, save in the records of the past, the people whom they held for seventy years in thrall are not only in existence still, but have the control of the secret springs of the world, and are destined to play a great part in its future history. Amid the removing of those things which could be shaken, because they were made by the wit or power of man, they have received a kingdom that could not be shaken—the kingdom of moral force, of character, of spiritual power.

This summons for an Exodus rings out to the Church of the Living God from the heavenly watchers. "I heard another voice from heaven," says the seer, "saying, 'Come forth out of her, My people, that ye be not partakers of her sins, and that ye receive not of her plagues.'" And in the words that follow there is an evident reference to the overthrow of Babylon, with an application to the Godless system of human society which confronts the Church in every age. In the early centuries it was represented by the Roman Empire; now it is present in the spirit of the world. The race of Babel-builders is not extinct. By his intellect and energy man is still endeavouring to rear a structure, independently of God; to make himself a name; and defy the waters of Time's deluge from sweeping away his work. All human imaginings, strivings, energisings, man's ceaseless activities, the outcome of human life, apart from the Spirit of God, constitute a fabric as real as that of Babel, or Babylon the Great; though no material fabric arises as its visible memorial.

From all this we are bidden to "come out and be separate." "Love not the world, neither the things that are in the world." "Touch no unclean thing." Let the spirit of a Divine love burn out the spirit of worldliness and self-hood. Come out—out from all fellowship with iniquity; out from all communion with darkness; out from all concord with Belial; out from partnership with unbelievers! Beyond Babylon lies the desert which must be traversed ere Jerusalem is reached, and we dread the privations through which we may be called to pass. The fear of these withheld large numbers of the Jews from obeying the edict of Cyrus. They remained in the land of their captivity till they lost their autonomy, and became the people of the Dispersion.

Let no such fear withhold thee, O Christian soul! It may seem as though the desert were to be traversed by thee, without break or intermission for many a weary year. But take heart! He will lead thee through the deserts; He will cause waters to flow from the rocks; He will cleave the rock, and the waters shall gush out. Supplies of which thou hast no conception shall surprise thee with their fitness and abundance. Thy track shall be marked with flowers and trees, glades where now are wastes, wells where now are the dunes of the desert. The time is fulfilled. Thy discipline is complete. The year of thy redemption is come. Go ye forth from the captivity which has so long held thee, to a freer, nobler, diviner life.

13

A POLISHED SHAFT

"The best men, doing their best,
Know peradventure least of what they do:
Men usefullest in the world are simply used;
The nail that holds the wood must pierce it first,
And He alone who wields the hammer sees
The work advanced by the earliest blow. Take heart!"

E. B. Browning

(Isaiah 49:2)

O isles of Greece, famed as the home of verse and song, ye were never summoned to listen to a voice so sweet as that which speaks in these words! Not Sappho, nor Homer himself, so well deserved your heed. And you, ye people of the world, though the speech be that of one of your obscurest tribes, an alien in a land of strangers, and itself falling into disuse, yet it contains words, which, once heard, shall be absorbed into all your many tongues, and recited in every dialect and language, the world over: "Listen, O Isles, unto Me; and hearken, ye peoples from far!"

And who is this that speaks in the Hebrew tongue, and presumes to address the world as his audience? We had thought the Jew-speech too exclusive, too conservative, too intolerant of strangers, to care to make itself heard beyond the limits of Judaism. The Jews have no dealings with the Samaritans. To the Jewish mind, Gentiles are dogs beneath the table. Whence these world-wide sympathies? Whence this sudden interest in the great family of man? Ah! these are the words of the Messiah, the ideal Jew; speaking in the name of the elect race, and representing its genius, not as warped by human prejudice, but as God intended it to be. "*He* said unto me, Thou art My servant; Israel, in whom I will be glorified."

There can be no doubt that this is the true way of considering these noble words. They were expressly referred to Jesus Christ by his greatest apostle on one of the most memorable occasions in his career. The little synagogue at Antioch was crowded to its doors. All the city was eager to hear the stranger, who had dropped down, so to speak, "from the snows of the Taurus." But this seriously affected the Jews, with their proud susceptibilities, and galled their pride. "They were filled with jealousy, contradicted the things which were spoken by Paul and Barnabas, and blasphemed." After a while the preacher realised that the terms of his commission did not require him to expend his words on those who, at every syllable, refused them; so he suddenly changed his note. He had made an offer of eternal life, which had been rejected with disdain; there was nothing left but to turn to the Gentiles, and he quoted the climax words of this paragraph in defence of the course he thereupon adopted. 'For so hath the Lord commanded us, saying, I have set thee for a light of the Gentiles, that thou shouldest be for salvation unto the uttermost part of the earth" (Acts 13:47, R.V.).

But, it may be asked, how can words, so evidently addressed to Israel, be appropriated, with equal truth, to Jesus Christ? To reply to this in full would take us too far afield. It is sufficient here to say that He was the epitome and personification of all that was noblest and divinest in Judaism. When, in spite of all that they had suffered in their exile, they for a second time failed to realise or fulfil their great mission to the world; when under the reign of Pharisee and Scribe they settled down into a nation of legalists, casuists, and hair-splitting ritualists—He assumed the responsiblities which they had evaded, and fulfilled them by the Gospel He spoke and the Church He formed. In the mission of Jesus, the heart of Judaism unfolded itself. What He was and did, the whole nation ought to have been and done. As the white flower on the stalk, He revealed the essential nature of the root. The very life of Jesus had a striking similarity to the history of the chosen people; and, therefore, Matthew with perfect propriety applies to Him a text, which Hosea wrote to the entire nation: "Joseph arose and took the young child and his mother by night, and departed into Egypt, and was there until the death of Herod; that it might be fulfilled which was spoken by the Lord through the prophet, saying, Out of Egypt did I call My Son" (Hos. 11:1 ; Matt. 2:14, 15, R.V.).

We are justified, therefore, in referring this paragraph to the Lord Jesus, as the ideal servant of God. And we may get some useful teaching as to the conditions of the loftiest and best service which, following his steps, we may render to his Father and our Father, to his God and ours.

(1) THE QUALIFICATIONS OF THE IDEAL SERVANT.—(1) *A holy motherhood*. "The Lord hath called me from the womb." The greatest and best of men have confessed their indebtedness to their mothers ; and not a few have, without doubt, enshrined in their character, and wrought out in their life, inspirations which had thrilled their mothers' natures from early girlhood. It is from their mothers that men get their souls. Many an obscure woman has ruled the world through the child in which her noblest self has been reproduced in masculine deeds and words. Rachel in Joseph ; Jochebed in Moses ; Hannah in Samuel ; Elizabeth in John the Baptist ; Monica in Augustine ; the mother of the Wesleys in her illustrious sons. With all reverence we say it, Mary of Nazareth has attained an influence which the Church of Rome could never give her, through her Son who rules the ages. We know that in Him the male and female blend in perfect symmetry ; and yet sometimes we think, in the human side of this wondrous nature, we trace the Virgin Mother—her delicate and quick sympathy ; her keen appreciation of beauty ; her reverent and accurate knowledge of the Old Testament Scriptures.

To make a man, God begins with his mother. How necessary it is, then, that young girls should be carefully trained to lofty thoughts and pure imaginings, that shall afterwards reappear in the strongest, fairest characters ; and how important it is that young women should carefully watch their hearts, restraining what is vain and evil, and reaching out after whatsoever things are true, just, pure, lovely, and of good report, not only in outward seeming, but in the inner chambers of the heart: for there the formative influences are ever brooding and maturing.

Few of us realise the immense importance attaching to the education of girls. Those who bear the children make our times. She that rocks the cradle rules the world.

The Zenanas of India must be taken for Christ before that great continent will yield to the Gospel. Any one, therefore, that can influence women by speech or pen, by education or example, has an almost unrivalled power over the destinies of our race. It is only a shallow and superficial critic who will sneer at a congregation of ser-vant-girls. The tendency of the present day notwith-standing, the highest function of woman is to give noble children to the world; in this she gives herself, and for this all education and environment should prepare her.

(2) *Incisive speech.* "He hath made my mouth like a sharp sword." Speech is the most God-like faculty in man. Christ did not scruple to be called the Word or Speech of God. "The tongue of man," says Carlyle, "is a sacred organ. Man himself is definable in philosophy as an incarnate word; the word not there, you have no man there either, but a phantasm instead." At the bid-ding of the human voice conceptions of beauty and thought emerge, darkness is dispelled, truth is unfolded, resolutions are born, inspirations conceived, crusades set on foot. Before the voice of man the lower creation trembles; and with his voice man joins in the ascriptions of adoration and praise which are ever arising around the eternal throne.

This regal faculty is God's chosen organ for announc-ing and establishing his Kingdom over the earth. He uses silence, the uncomplaining passivity of the down-trodden and oppressed; He uses deeds, erecting vast structures as their monument; He uses books, the seed-baskets of thought: but He especially uses words. When John was cast into prison, Jesus came preaching. He opened his mouth and taught; He bade his disciples go into all the world and preach his Gospel to every creature. By the foolishness of preaching, it is God's pleasure to save them that believe. And so long as the pulpit is con-tent to be the mouthpiece of the living Spirit, it cannot be superseded by the press.

Our mouth must be surrendered to God, that He may implant there the sharp two-edged sword that proceeds from his own lips (Rev. 1:16). We must see to it that we do not speak our own words, nor think our own thoughts; but open our mouths wide, that He may fill

87

them with the Word of God, which is quick, and power-
ful, and sharper than any two-edged sword (Heb. 4:12).
"He hath made"—precious words, denoting on the one
hand the submissive attitude which yields itself to receive ;
and on the other, the touch of the living God, who promises to be with the mouth, and teach what we should
say. Who does not want to speak as Peter did, when, on
the day of Pentecost, many were pricked in their heart?
—or as Stephen did, when, in the Sanhedrin, we are told
that his opponents were cut to the heart by his incisive
speech? We do not want to give mere sword-play to delight the eyes of our hearers ; but to pierce to the dividing asunder of soul and spirit, so that those who are unbelieving may be convicted and judged, and the secrets
of their hearts revealed.

(3) *Seclusion.* "In the shadow." We must all go there
sometimes. The glare of the daylight is too brilliant ;
our eyes become injured, and unable to discern the
delicate shades of colour, or appreciate neutral tints—
the shadowed chamber of sickness ; the shadowed house
of mourning ; the shadowed life from which the sunlight
has gone. But, fear not!—it is the shadow of God's hand.
He is leading thee. There are lessons that can only be
learnt there. The photograph of his face can only be
fixed in the dark chamber. But do not suppose that He
has cast thee aside. Thou art still in his quiver ; He has
not flung thee away as a worthless thing. He is only keeping thee close till the moment comes when He can send
thee most swiftly and surely on some errand in which
He will be glorified. Oh, shadowed solitary ones, remember how closely the quiver is bound to the warrior, within
easy reach of the hand, and guarded jealously!

(4) *Freed from rust.* "A polished shaft." Weapons of
war soon deteriorate. A breath of damp leaves its cor-
roding mark ; and the rust shows where the metal is slowly
burning away. In archery, a rusted arrow-point will fail
to penetrate, and glance away from the target ; and so,
in war, a sword or spear corroded by rust would not
cleave its way through helmet or shield.

Rust can best be removed by sandpaper or the file.
Similarly we must be kept bright and clean. There must
be no rust on our hearts resulting from inconsistency or
permitted sin. To keep us from thus deteriorating is

88

God's perpetual aim; and for this purpose He uses the fret of daily life, the chafe of small annoyances, the wear and tear of irritating tempers and vexing circumstances. Nothing great or crushing, but many things that gall and vex—these are the sandpaper and the file that God perpetually employs to guard against whatever would blunt the edge or diminish the effect of our work.

(2) APPARENT FAILURE.—"But I said, I have laboured in vain; I have spent my strength for nought and vanity." This heart-break seems inevitable to God's most gifted and useful servants. It is in part the result of nervous overstrain; as, after the great day of Carmel, Elijah threw himself down beneath the juniper-tree, and asked that he might die. But in part it results from the expanding compassion of the soul, becoming aware how little one man can do to mitigate the anguish of the world. We are so long in learning how to work, we have to unlearn so much, we have to return from so many paths that lead nowhere; it is already afternoon when we commence to use the experience we have gotten, and pursue the right tracks that we have at last discovered; then after an hour or two of bright labour, our strength begins to wane, the sun of our brief day to near the western hills, and all is over. The night has come, in which no man can work. How often we thought our mothers hard when in childhood they said that we must come in and go to bed. And the most strenuous workers will feel like that when God calls them home; unless they are very tired and lonely because so many of their companions have left them—*then* they will perhaps be glad.

The heart is capable of infinite yearnings and compassion, while the physical strength is limited and finite. Evil is so hydra-headed and Protean. The bias to evil in each generation is so strong and inveterate. The restless sea of which the prophet spoke is so constantly sweeping away the embankments and walls reared against its incursions. It seems so impossible to reach the root, the secret spring, the heart. The circle of light only makes the surrounding darkness more pitch-black. What can one weak man effect against such overwhelming odds!

There are three sources of consolation. First, that failure will not forfeit the bright smile of the Master's welcome nor the reward of his Judgment-seat. He judges

89

righteously; and rewards, not according to results, but to faithfulness. "Yet, *surely*, my judgment is with the Lord, and my recompense with my God" (4). Secondly, the soul leans more heavily upon God: "my God is become my strength" (5). Thirdly, we turn to prayer. How sweetly God refers to this, saying, "In an acceptable time have I answered thee, and in a day of salvation have I helped thee" (8).

Thus God deals with us all. He is compelled to take us to the back side of the desert, where we sit face to face with the wreck of our fairest hopes. There He teaches us, as He only can, weaning us from creature-confidence, and taking pride from our hearts. Then from the stump of the tree, hewn almost to the ground, comes the scion of a new life, which fulfils the promise that seemed for ever annulled.

(3) ULTIMATE SUCCESS.—When Jesus died, *failure* seemed written across his life-work. A timid handful of disciples was all that remained of the crowds that had thronged his pathway, and they seemed disposed to go back to their fishing-boats. Man despised Him; the nation abhorred Him; and the rulers set Him at nought. But that very cross, which man deemed His supreme disgrace and dethronement, has become the stepping-stone of universal dominion. Israel shall yet be gathered, and the Gentile Church become as the sand of the sea.

Thus it may be with some who peruse this page. They are passing through times of barrenness, and disappointment, and suffering. But let them remember that the Lord is faithful (7). He will not suffer one word to fail, one seed to be lost, one effort to prove abortive, one life to be wasted. And *because* of this, they shall be preserved; lands which they have discovered and cultivated shall teem with men; measures that they have concerted shall effect the liberation of the blind and the enslaved; trees they have planted shall become forests, and beneficially affect the climate of the world. Yea, these shall be light things, to be succeeded by greater and yet greater, as the circle of their influence widens through the universe, and the throb of their life reacts on coming ages.

Whilst Christ from the throne of his glory sees the travail of his soul, He is assuredly satisfied; and when, from the hills of glory, as from another Pisgah, we be-

hold the results of our lifework, the way by which God
led us, and answered our prayers, and blessed our feeble
attempts to serve Him, we shall forget the pain and disappointment amid the gladness of the overwhelming and
transporting spectacle.

14

THE LOVE THAT WILL NOT LET US GO

"My God, Thou art all Love!
Not one poor minute 'scapes Thy breast
But brings a favour from above—
And in this Love—I rest."

Herbert

(Isaiah 49:16)

This chapter is strewn with assurances to the chosen
people on the eve of their return from Babylon. They
were timid, and reluctant to quit the familiar scenes of
their captivity; they dreaded the dangers and privations
of the journey back; and questioned whether the great
empire of their captors would ever let them go, or permit
their city to arise from her ruins. Therefore Jehovah's
voice takes on a tone of unusual tenderness, and speaks
as He only can. Let us heed his successive assurances
of comfort and compassion, "for the Lord hath comforted his people, and will have compassion upon his
afflicted."

(1) HE WILL LEAD WITH A SHEPHERD'S CARE.—The pre-
vailing characteristic of the early Hebrews was pastoral;
"Jacob kept sheep." The patriarchs of the nation were
"the stateliest shepherds of all time." Its ideal king and
its earliest prophet were taken from following the flocks.
The imagery of the flock, therefore, deeply dyed the
national speech, and enriched it with striking analogies.
The king, and every true leader, and above all, Jehovah,
was called the Shepherd of his people. "We are the sheep

of his pasture." This is the conception that underlies these tender assurances: "They shall not hunger nor thirst; neither shall the heat nor sun smite them: for He that hath mercy on them shall lead them, even by the springs of water shall He guide them" (10).

The life of the eastern shepherd is very different from anything we are accustomed to in these northern climes. He occupies some rocky coign of vantage, whence he looks out on his sheep thinly scattered over the moorland; or leads them down to the valleys with their strips of green pasture and waters of rest; or conducts them through gloomy gorges where wild beasts have their lairs, they huddling close to his heels, wakeful, far-sighted, weather-beaten, armed with club and staff, always thoughtful for the defenceless, helpless creatures of his charge. You detect the accent of the true shepherd in Jacob's excuse for not accompanying the rapid march of Esau and his warriors. "The flocks and herds with me give suck, and if they overdrive them one day, all the flocks will die. I will lead on softly, according to the pace of the cattle that is before me."

All this, and much more, is summed up in the exceedingly beautiful words, "He that hath mercy on them shall lead them." What comfort is here! He knows our frame. He is touched with the feeling of our infirmities; He will not over-drive us. He will go before and lead us, but He will suit his pace to ours. The longest day's march shall be adjusted to our capacities. The severest strain shall not overtax our powers. However rough and difficult the path, ever remember that thou art being led by Him who has mercy on thee. Hunger and thirst will be impossible for those who abide in his care and fellowship. Art thou enveloped in shadow? It is only lest heat or sun smite thee. Is the descent swift and precipitous? It is only that He may bring thee to the springs of water of life (Rev. 7:17).

Do not murmur, Christian soul; but ever repeat to thyself, like a sweet, soft refrain, "He that hath mercy on me is leading me; even to springs of water is He guiding me. Sing, O heavens; oh, be joyful, O earth; and break forth into singing, O mountains!"

(2) HE WILL MAKE OBSTACLES SERVE HIS PURPOSE.—"I will make all my mountains a way." Mountains are pro-

hibitory. The student of the geography of Palestine cannot fail to be impressed with the strong barricade of mountains with which God fenced in the Land of Promise on its southern frontier. "South of Beersheba, before the level desert is reached, and the region of roads from Arabia to Egypt and Philistia, there lie sixty miles of mountainous country, mostly disposed in steep ridges running east and west. The vegetation even after rain is very meagre, and in summer totally disappears. No great route leads, or ever has led, through this district. Its steep and haggard ridges are utterly inaccessible."

Similarly, the mountains of Switzerland have sheltered liberty, and those of Afghanistan have made conquest difficult to impossibility. There were great mountains between Israel and home, yet God does not say that He would remove them; but that they should form a pathway, as though contributing to the ease and speed of the return. "I will make all my mountains a way."

We all have mountains in our lives. There are people and things that threaten to bar our progress in the Divine life. That trying temperament; that large family; those heavy claims; that uncongenial occupation; that thorn in the flesh; that daily cross. We think that if only these were removed, we might live purer, tenderer, holier lives; and often we pray for their removal. O fools and slow of heart! These are the very conditions of achievement; they have been put into our life as the means to the very graces and virtues for which we have been so long praying.

Thou hast prayed for patience through long years, but there is something that tries thee beyond endurance; thou hast fled from it, evaded it, accounted it an unsurmountable obstacle to the desired attainment, and supposed that its removal would secure thy immediate deliverance and victory. Not so! Thou wouldest only gain the cessation of temptations to impatience. But this would not be patience. Patience can only be acquired through just such trials as now seem unbearable. Go back, and submit thyself. Claim to be a partaker in the patience of Jesus. Meet thy trials in Him. Thus shall the mountains that stand between thee and thy promised land become thy way to it.

Note the comprehensiveness of this promise. "I will

93

make *all* my mountains a way." There is nothing in life which harasses and annoys that may not become subservient to the highest ends. No exception can obtain against this great though small word, *all*. Consider also that possessive pronoun. They are *His* mountains. He put them there.

But do not forget that the promise is in the future tense. "I *will* make." We do not see the pathway from afar ; but in the distance only a tumbled mass of rocks. The keenest sight cannot discern the point at which the threading path shall intersect them. But why anticipate? We know that God will not fail his promise. "He understandeth the way thereof and knoweth the place thereof ; for He looketh to the ends of the earth, and seeth under the whole heaven." And when we come to the foot of the mountains, we shall find the way.

(3) GOD'S LOVE IS MORE THAN MOTHERHOOD.—Many devout but misguided souls have placed the Virgin Mother on a level with God, and worship her, because they think that woman is more tender, more patient, more forgiving than man. "The love of woman" was David's high-water-mark of love. And of woman's love, none is so pure, so unselfish, so full of patient brooding pity, as a mother's. Oh, heart of woman, it is in the first ecstasy of motherhood that thou art betrayed. Bending over the laughing babe, returning thy kisses and sallies, in an ecstasy of delight ; soothing the suffering and wakeful one with snatches of lullabies and broken bits of baby-talk ; watching beside the little flickering taper that will soon go out, leaving thee cold and dark ; giving nights and days without a murmur or regret ; prepared to surrender sleep, food, life, for thy child—that is what motherhood means. And that love follows us through life ; often repelled and unrequited, it lingers near us in prayers and tears and holy yearnings ; at the first symptom of illness, or summons of distress, it hurries to our side ; it schemes and plans ; it will stand by the felon in the dock, and hunt for a girl through Sodom ; it sheds over our graves tears not less scalding than those of husband or wife.

Such love is God's. Indeed it is a ray from his heart. If a mother's love is but the ray, what must His heart be! But there is sometimes a failure in motherhood. "They may forget." Maddened with frenzy, soddened with drink, flushed with unholy passion, infatuated with the giddy round of gaiety, a woman has been known to forget her sucking child. Indeed, as is recorded of the siege of Samaria, there have been times when women have stayed their hunger with the flesh of their children. But God can never so forget.

We may fall into the slough, so that our dearest will disown us ; but He will not forget. We may become scarred and sin-pocked, so as to be almost unrecognisable ; but He will not forget. We may be away in the far country so long that the candle will cease to burn at night in the window of the most faithful friend ; but He will not forget. The fires on all human altars may have burnt to white ash ; but his love will be what it was when first we knew Him.

(4) GOD TREASURES THE THOUGHT OF HIS OWN.—The Orientals have a custom of tattooing the name of beloved friends on the hand. That is the reference here ; but notice the emphasis. Not the name of Zion merely ; but Zion herself, the city where David dwelt, and Solomon built his temple. This was engraved on the Divine hand. Yes, child of God, thou art photographed where God must ever behold thee, on his hands, on his heart. Thou art never for a moment out of his thought, nor hidden from his eye.

Not on one hand only, but on both. It is the plural in each case, "On the palms of my hands."

Not tattooed or photographed, the marks of which might be obliterated and obscured ; but graven. The graving tool was the spear, the nail, the cross. "Don't write there," said an urchin to a young exquisite scratching with a diamond on the window of a waiting-room. "Why not?" was the startled inquiry. "Because you can't rub it out," was the instant retort. Glass will not give up its inscriptions, nor the onyx stone its seal, nor the cameo its profile ; but sooner might they renounce their trust than the hands of Christ. "In the midst of the throne a Lamb as it had been slain." "He showed unto them his hands and his side."

Not Zion's ruins ; but her walls, as they were before Nebuchadnezzar broke them down—as they were meant to be. For fifty or sixty years those walls had been in ruins. Nehemiah tells us that the *debris* forbade the beast he rode to pass, when he made by moonlight his first sad tour of inspection. Sanballat mocked about the heaps of rubbish. But God did not keep those ruins in mind, associated as they were with Israel's follies and sins. Zion's *walls* were ever before Him. Our ideal self; what we are in Jesus; what we long to be in our best moments; what we will be when grace has perfected its work and we are comely in the comeliness He shall put upon us —this is the ineffaceable conception of us that is ever before God.

What a constrast between Zion's wail about being forsaken and forgotten, and God's tender regard! So the believer, considering the desolations of his soul and the ruins of past joys, is apt to think himself a castaway. But it is not so. At the time of his deepest despair, God is thinking of him, as a mother of her first-born babe; and his need is ever before Him.

(5) GOD'S LOVE IS STRONG ENOUGH TO CARRY OUT ITS PURPOSE.—"Shall the prey be taken from the mighty, or the lawful captive delivered?" (24). Such is the question of despondency, asked by Israel, from the heart of the mighty empire, in which she was a helpless captive.

But Jehovah had well calculated his resources. Let but his hand be uplifted, and his people would be restored, brought back to their land by the solicitude of kings and queens. Do not consider the difficulties of thy deliverance, nor brood over past failure and mighty foes; look away from these to Him. He will become thy Greatheart, thy Champion; He will espouse thy cause and carry it through; He will show Himself strong on thy behalf. "Thus saith the Lord, Even the captives of the mighty shall be taken away, and the prey of the terrible shall be delivered; for I will contend with him that contendeth with thee, and I will save thy children."

(6) GOD'S LOVE WILL NOT PUT AWAY.—When the Jew put away his wife, he gave her a bill of divorcement (Mark 10:4). Without this piece of writing the divorce was not complete; and the husband could take his wife again without blame. Israel, away in the land of exile, thinks herself a divorced wife. She does not say as much;

but she thinks, she fears it. Jehovah answers those unspoken questionings, by reminding her that she cannot
produce a bill of divorce. "Thus saith the Lord, Where
is the bill of your mother's divorcement, wherewith I
have put her away?" He may well ask where it is: He
knows that it cannot be found, for He has never given
it.

God cannot divorce those whom He has once taken
into covenant with Himself. Backsliding, rebellious,
and faithless they may be; but they are his still. Though
the universe be ransacked, the bill of divorce cannot be
produced. The devil himself cannot confront us with it.
And the love of God will yet win back the souls on which
it has set itself. In a little wrath He hid his face for a
moment; but with everlasting kindness will He forgive
and gather and have mercy.

15

WORDS IN SEASON FOR THE WEARY

"Thou knowest, not alone as God, all-knowing;
  As Man, our mortal weakness Thou hast proved:
On earth, with purest sympathies o'erflowing,
  O Saviour, Thou hast wept, and Thou hast loved:
And love and sorrow still to Thee may come,
And find a hiding-place, a rest, a home."

H. L. L.

(Isaiah 50:4)

Ever since the world began, men have been weary.
"Weary" denotes a class to which a multitude belong
that no man can number, of every nation, kindred, tribe,
and people. *Physical* weariness—of the slave on the
march; of the toiler in the sweating den; of the seam-
stress working far into the night by the wasting taper;
of the mother worn with watching her sick child. *Mental*
weariness—when the fancy can no longer summon at

will images of beauty; and the intellect refuses to follow another argument, master another page, or cast up another column. *Heart* weariness—waiting in vain for the word so long expected but unspoken; for the returning step of the prodigal; for the long-delayed letter. The weariness of *the inner conflict* of striving day by day against the selfishness and waywardness of the soul on which prolonged resistance makes so slight an impression. The weariness of the *Christian worker,* worn by the perpetual chafe of human sorrow, sin, and need.

If only we could make one brilliant assault on the powers of evil, which should for ever quell their might, so that they would perforce retreat, leaving the field with us—who would not accept it as the most blessed gift of God? But, instead of this, we are engaged in a conflict which is tedious, incessant, and terribly wearing. If we defeat our enemy to-day, he will be ready to meet us to-morrow with equal force. If we conquer him in one thing, he will straightway disguise himself in another. Thus beneath the long ordeal, heart and flesh fail; and we sigh for the place over whose portal Christ has written, "Come unto Me, all ye that labour and are heavy laden, and I will give you rest."

Thus, in one way or another, all souls at some part of their life get weary. There is nothing novel in this; but the novelty, the great novelty, consists in the infinite care that God takes of the weary. There is nothing like it outside the Bible, and the literature to which it has given birth. Man hears with composure that scores of weary ones have fallen out of the march of human life, and lie stretched on the scorching sand, doomed to expire of fatigue and thirst. God, on the other hand, the High and Holy One, inhabiting Eternity, stoops to the need of the weakling; expends his care on the lame, halt, maimed, and blind; adopts into his family those who had been rejected for their deformities and ugliness; gathers up the broken fragments; tills the sterile ground; ransacks the highways and byways for the waifs and strays whom no one invites to his board; and is perpetually engaged in brooding over each weary heart with its sore, its tears, its yearnings, its despair. This God is our God for ever and ever, unrivalled in his tender pity, the God of the fatherless and the widow.

But the deep tenderness of God for every tired atom

of humanity had been hidden from our knowledge, had it not been for the Good Servant who speaks in these paragraphs, and who combines the form of the Servant and equality with Jehovah. No one ever comforted the weary as He did. He could not look upon a great multitude, distressed and scattered as sheep not having a shepherd, without being moved with compassion towards them, and beginning to speak as only He could. How many weary souls did He sustain with his words (R.V.); to how many did he speak a word in season (A.V)! Ask Him, speaking after the manner of men, whence He derived this matchless power; and He will answer, "The Lord God gave it Me. In his great love for weary souls everywhere, He raised Me up to be their Shepherd. Through days and nights, He taught Me, wakening Me morning by morning to some new lesson of sympathy and mercy, comforting Me amid the assaults of my foes and the darkness of dark hours, that I might be able to comfort others with the comfort wherewith I Myself had been comforted by my Father."

We are brought then to consider the education, resolution, vindication, and entreaty of the true Servant of Jehovah. Himself God over all.

(1) THE EDUCATION OF THE DIVINE SERVANT.—We must notice the difference between the authorised version and the new. In the one, "the Lord God hath given Me the tongue of the learned, that I should know." In the other, "of them that are taught"—or, as the margin reads, "of disciples." The thought being that the Lord Jesus in his human life was a pupil in the school of human pain, under the tutelage of his Father, of whom He said, "I do nothing of Myself, but as the Father taught Me I speak these things." "I am a Man that hath told you the truth which I heard from God" (John 8:28, 40). This is in keeping also with that marvellous word of the Epistle to the Hebrews, "Though He were a Son, yet learned He obedience by the things which He suffered; and, having been made perfect, He became unto all them that obey Him the Author of Eternal Salvation."

His education was by God Himself. "The Lord God hath given Me ... He wakeneth morning by morning ... The Lord God hath opened mine ear."

99

It was various. He passed through each class in the school of weariness. Being wearied with his journey, He sat by Sychar's well; they took Him, even as He was, in the ship; He looked up to Heaven and sighed, because of the pressure of human pain, and the obstinacy of unbelief; He suffered being tempted; He once cried in the bitterness of his soul, "How long shall I be with you, and suffer you?" He was glad when the hour came that He should go home to his Father. The waves of human sorrow broke over his tender heart, and though possessed of an inexhaustible patience, there was an incessant waste of the physical tissues, beneath which at last He fainted on the way to Calvary.

It was constant. "Morning by morning" the Father woke Him. After his brief snatch of sleep, amid the thyme of the hill-side, or in the storm of the fishing-smack, or on the couch that the sisters' love had spread for Him at Bethany, the Spirit touched and summoned Him to the new lesson of the fresh young day. Morning by morning He was awakened to learn, by the ever-changing circumstances of daily providence, some deeper phase of the world's suffering and its medicine. Would that we were quicker to detect that same awakening touch; and to learn the lessons taught by the circumstances of our lot as to the treatment of the weary and suffering.

It dealt with the season for administering comfort. "That I should know how to speak a word in season." It is not enough to speak the right word; you must speak it at the right moment, or it will be in vain. Many a word spoken out of season has fallen like a seed on the wayside to be devoured by birds; whilst the same word, uttered at the right time by a voice with less quality of tone, has been God's balm. It is not easy to know just when to speak to the weary. There are times when the nervous system is so overstrained that it cannot bear even the softest words. It is best then to be silent. A caress, a touch, or the stillness that breathes an atmosphere of calm, will then most quickly soothe and heal. This delicacy of perception can only be acquired in the school of suffering. Our Master knows when to speak, and when to be still, because He has graduated there.

It embraced the method. "That I should know *how*." The manner is as important as the season. A message of goodwill may be uttered with so little sympathy, and in tones so gruff and grating, that it will rebel. The psalmist speaks of words so soft that they do not break the head! The touch of the comforter must be that of the nurse on the fractured bone—of the mother with the frightened child. God knows how delicately strung our system is, and how it demands the gentle tread across the floor; movements like the fall of rose-petals on the grass; methods of perfect sympathy. All these *He* has provided, who made the snow descend in noiseless flakes, and the ocean break in silvery ripple on the sand. Thy King hath been trained to this; lo! He comes, meek and lowly, sitting on the ambling foal. He will not break the bruisèd reed, nor quench the smoking flax.

It seems to me as if the education of our High Priest has not ceased with his transference from this world of sorrow to the realm where weariness is never felt. His ministry to weary hearts through succeeding ages has made his eye more quick, his touch more delicate.

O weary soul! I have seen Him coming to thy help. The voice of the Shepherd lifts itself, calling thy name. He is searching for thee by crag, and brake, and torrent-bed. He knows just how to take thee. He will cast thee about IIis shoulders rejoicing, and so bring thee home.

(2) HIS RESOLUTION.—From the first, Jesus knew that He must die. The Lord God poured the full story into his opened ear. With all other men, death is the close of their life; with Christ it was the object. We die because we were born; Christ was born that He might die. From his birth the shadow of the Cross fell athwart his soul, as the young pigeons shed their blood for Him in the temple courts. To Nicodemus He said, "The Son of Man must be lifted up." The scene in the halls of Caiaphas, Herod and Pilate, were as present to his prevision as the scenes of the past are to our memory! Frequently He took his disciples apart, and told them that the Son of Man would be delivered into the hands of men who would handle Him shamefully—mock, spit upon, scourge, and kill Him (Mark 10:34). But though He anticipated all, yet He was not rebellious, neither turned away back.

On one occasion towards the close of his earthly career,

101

when the fingers of the dial-plate were pointing to the near fulfilment of the time, we are told He set his face steadfastly to go to Jerusalem. What heroism was here! Men sometimes speak of Christ as if He were effeminate and weak, deficient in manly courage, and remarkable only for passive virtues. But such conceptions are refuted by the indomitable resolution which sets its face like a flint, and knew that it would not be ashamed.

Note the voluntariness of Christ's surrender. The martyr dies because he cannot help it; Christ died because He chose. He laid down his life of Himself; no one took it from Him. He might have been rebellious and turned away backward, or called for twelve legions of angels, or pinned his captors to the ground by the out-flashing of his inherent God-head; but He forbore. Listen to his words, as He treads the wine-press alone! "Thy will, not mine be done." It is this which throws his resolution into such clear relief. It is this that stirs our hearts with admiration and devotion, as we see Him deliberately giving his back to the smiters, and his cheeks to them that pluck off the hair, and exposing to shame and spitting the face that angels gaze on with unceasing reverence, and from which, some day, heaven and earth will flee away.

It has been thought that the opened ear refers to something more than the pushing back of the flowing Oriental locks in order to utter the secret of coming sorrow. It is supposed to have some reference to the ancient Jewish custom of boring the ear of the slave to the doorpost of the master's house. Under this metaphor it is held that our Lord chose with keen sympathy the service of the Father, and elected all that it might involve, because He loved Him and would not go out free. The images may be combined. Be it only remembered that He knew and chose all that would come upon Him, and that the fetters which bound Him to the cross were those of undying love to us and of burning passion for the Father's glory.

(3) HIS VINDICATION.—"He is near that justifieth Me." These are words upon which Jesus may have stayed Himself through those long hours of trial. The Father who sent Him was with Him. Not for a moment did He leave Him alone. God was near. The triumph with which Paul

quotes these words of the justification in which the soul which has made Jesus its refuge, is privileged to robe itself, is but the sigh of an Æolian harp, contrasted with the peal of an organ, in comparison with the exultation that filled the heart of the Son of Man as He contemplated his vindication by his Father before all worlds.

Who is he that condemneth Me? we hear Him say; "it is God that justifieth!" Justification being used here in the sense of vindication, not, as with us, of the imputation of righteousness.

They said that He was the friend of publicans and sinners. God has justified Him by showing that if He associates with such, it is to make them martyrs and saints.

They said that He was mad. God has justified Him by making his teaching the illumination of the noblest and wisest of the race.

They said He had a devil. But God has justified Him by giving Him power to cast out the devil and bind him with a mighty chain.

They said that He blasphemed when He called Himself the Son of God. But God has justified Him by raising Him to the right hand of power, so that He will come in the clouds of heaven, with power and great glory.

They said He would destroy the temple and the commonwealth of Israel. God has justified Him in shedding the influence of the Hebrew people through all the nations of the world, and making their literature, their history, their conceptions dominant. Where are those who have condemned the Lord Jesus? Their books rot on the top shelves of libraries in undisturbed dust. Their names are only remembered as quoted in the apologetics of the defenders of the Christian faith. Their memory has not survived moth-eating time. Behold, they have all waxed old as doth a garment! The moth has eaten them up. They have passed away as an ill dream; whilst the exalted Saviour is enthroned daily in more hearts, with more enthusiasm, and with growing appreciation. His throne is established for ever and ever. Oh, do not be afraid of the wrath of man, thou child of the King! for "the moth shall eat them up as a garment, and the worm shall eat them like wool." The fate that has overtaken the adversaries of thy King shall overtake thine (51: 8). Only be still, as He was; set thy face as a flint; commit thy cause to God; count not on thy protestations, but upon his vindications—and He shall bring forth thy righteousness as the light, and thy judgment as the noonday. He will help thee; fear not! thou shalt not be confounded.

(4) HIS APPEAL.—To obey the Lord's Servant is equivalent to fearing the Lord. He who does the one must do the other. What is this but to proclaim his Deity? Those who are thus designated, who, because they fear God, brave the wrath of man, who dare to obey the voice of the Servant as the voice of his Father, are often called to walk through darkness, where there is no light. It may be the valley of the shadow of death, or the garden of Gethsemane, or the midday-midnight of Calvary. But from the depth of his own experience the Divine Servant counsels such, that they should trust where they cannot see, and stay themselves upon God.

Do not stand still, or sit down, or go back, or despair; but keep right onward, believing that the growing light on the fringe of the darkness heralds the advent of the morning. God will help thee. Thou shalt not be ashamed. Set thy face as a flint. Let thy feet hold the appointed track.

The temptation at such an hour is to kindle a fire, and to gird oneself about with firebrands (R.V.); but these die out after a brief sparkle, leaving the darkness more intense. Then with dazzled eye, the Godless soul stumbles in the thicket, and is flung headlong into the pit of destruction. "This shall ye have of Mine hand, ye shall lie down in sorrow." How awful such a lot must be!—to lie down in the dying moment with sorrow for a wasted life behind, and a dark eternity before. Oh, abandon your fire with its sparks; and avail yourselves of the light of the Word of God, as a lamp to your feet, and a light to your path, until the day dawn and the Daystar arise on your hearts!

16

THE THRICE "HEARKEN"

"Be still, sad soul! lift thou no passionate cry,
But spread the desert of thy being bare
To the full searching of the All-seeing eye ;
Wait!—and through dark misgiving, blank despair,
God will come down in pity, and fill the dry
Dead place with light, and life, and vernal air."

J. C. Shairp

(Isaiah 51:1-8.)

These paragraphs are exceedingly dramatic. We become conscious that we are approaching a revelation of unparalleled sublimity which shall be in Scripture what heart or brain or eye is in the human body. The encasing of each of these in strong protecting walls convinces the most superficial of the priceless value of the treasure they are formed to guard. And as we consider the thrice "Hearken" of this paragraph, and the thrice "Awake" of the succeeding one, we realise that we are entering the presence-chamber of the profoundest mysteries of love and redemption.

Travellers who have visited the ruined temples of Egypt describe the splendours of their approaches. Long corridors, guarded by the imperturbable and stupendous statues of defunct deities, avenues of pillars, and the shadow of imposing façades and porticoes—everything that human art could devise prepared the mind for the magnificence of the inner shrine. Similarly, as we read these chapters, our mind becomes educated, our eye focused and adjusted, our sense of perspective trained, that with hushed and awful dread we may pass in to worship before the dying Man of Calvary.

The people, notwithstanding the promises of deliverance from exile and the summons to depart, seemed unable to believe that they were destined to become again a great nation, or that Zion's wastes would be repaired!

Already the Servant of Jehovah had sought to answer their anxious questionings, and reassure them by announcing a love that would not let them go. And in these words He betakes Himself to the same strain. He prefaces his words by the thrice repeated "Hearken," addressed to those "that follow after righteousness" in the first verse; and to "those that know righteousness" in the seventh. These are always the stages in the development of character: they that follow presently possess.

(1) THE LESSONS OF RETROSPECT.—It is wholesome for the pillar, with its fluted column and decorated coronal, to look down to the quarry whence it came; and for us all to look back to the lowliness and obscurity of our origin. Such considerations deepen our humility, and augment our thankfulness for the grace of God which has made us what we are.

Remember, O man, the rock of the first Adam, the pit of selfhood, passion, murder, out of which thou wast taken! She who plucked the tempting fruit in violation of her Maker's word was thy mother; and he who cast the blame on her and preferred the indulgence of the flesh to the regimen of the spirit was thy father. For thy brother thou must take Cain, and for thy sister Rahab. Thou knowest the strong affinities by which thou art bound to each of these. Thou canst not rid thyself of the features of the family likeness, nor wholly escape the betraying accent of the family speech! What has brought thee from such an origin, and made thee a pillar in the temple of God, but the grace which had no reason save itself, no measure save infinity? Boast not thyself. There is nothing in thee to account for such transformation. Render thy homage where it belongs, and reason, that if God has done so much, He can easily perfect it. If thou wert excavated, surely thou canst be shaped! If thou wert hewn, surely thou canst be polished! If thou wert justified, surely thou canst be sanctified! If, when an enemy, thou wert reconciled by the death of his Son, how much more, being reconciled, thou shalt be saved by his life!

It was for her encouragement that Israel was primarily directed to this retrospect. The nation was greatly reduced in numbers, and the Godly were but a handful. It seemed preposterous to suppose that they would ever attain to such prolific numbers as to rival the sands on the shore, or the stars of space. The tree had been so mercilessly cut down, and pruned, that they despaired of again beholding its spreading branches, laden with fruit. In answer to such forebodings the voice of inspiration cries, "Look back! Consider Abraham and Sarah. There was a time when they were the sole representatives of the Hebrew race; yet of them and of the one son of their old age sprang countless myriads. What little cause, then, is there for fear! Though you were reduced to a single aged pair, these might become the origin of a mighty nation! How much more is there reason for hope now that you may still be counted by your thousands!" "Look unto Abraham your father, and unto Sarah that bare you; for when he was but one I called him, and blessed him and made him many."

Let us recount the steps of Abraham's pruning, on which God lays stress in saying, "When he was but one, I called him."

He stood alone. First, Terah died, after having started with him for the Land of Promise, emblem of those who in old age start on the pilgrimage of faith and hope, not too much tied by the conservatism of nature, or the traditions of the past. Then Lot dropped away, and went down to Sodom; and it must have been difficult for the old man, as he saw the retreating forms of his camp followers, to be wholly unmoved. Then Sarah's scheme miscarried, and Hagar was thrust from his tents with her child. Lastly, his Isaac was laid upon the altar. By successive strokes the shadows grew deeper and darker; and he stood alone, face to face with God and his purpose. But the fire that burned in his heart rose higher, shone brighter, and has ignited myriads with its flame. You only need a spark to light a conflagration. Chicago was burned down by the upsetting of a tiny lamp. If there be heroic faith in one lonely heart, it shall spread to untold millions.

His faith was sorely tried. First by the long delay; then by the growing unlikelihood that he should have a child, since natural force was spent; then by the summons to offer Isaac on Mount Moriah: every test was applied to his power of endurance. To the end of his life he was a stranger and pilgrim, only seeing the prom-

107

ises from afar, and dying with an unfulfilled hope. He little realised the perfect work his patience was producing. He may not have understood how utterly God must reduce and cut us down before He can graft upon us his rarest fruit. He did not see that our proud flesh will glory, though it be of a strand, a smoking flax, a broken reed. To him the necessity for knife and fire was not so patent as to us. As we look back upon it all, we see that it could not have been otherwise. If the seed was to be a Divine gift to his faith, then nature herself must forfeit vitality and hope, that God might be all in all.

From Abraham I turn to thee, much-suffering believer, cut to the quick and to the roots, brought into the dust of death, stripped of reputation, wealth, prestige, the gifts and graces of oratory, faculty to command. Yet be of good cheer!—Abraham passed this way before thee. It is all part of a necessary process. Nothing has happened to hinder, but all to help thee to become the parent of a great spiritual progeny. Because of the destruction of nature, thou mayest reckon on the prolific abundance of grace.

His history is the type of God's dealings with men. Not once nor twice in the record of the Church the cause of truth has been entrusted to a tiny handful of defenders, who have deemed it forlorn or lost. The prophet has stood alone lamenting that he only was left. The dens and caves have sheltered the loyal but diminished few. Ragged, tattered, harried, exiled, these have gathered around the banner and followed it. Few of the mighty, noble, or learned have been called, and not many of the poor. But suddenly God has called out from some unlikely quarter one man, and it has seemed as though the dust were suddenly transformed into warriors, and truth sprang up from the dust as luxuriantly as grass after spring rains. Sir Walter Scott's picture of the apparently empty glens suddenly teeming with armed men at the sign of the chieftain has often had its counterpart in the great army which has arisen from the life, or words, or witness, of a single man.

It was so in the days of the Arian heresy, when Athanasius stood alone against the world for the deity of Christ. It was so at the Reformation, when Europe lay asleep under the soporific of the Papacy. It was so when first

108

the abolition of slavery began to be agitated. God has repeatedly shown that He has no taste for strong battalions; He chooses a Gideon, a Judas Maccabæus, a Luther, a Wilberforce. The history of the Church is largely a story of the lives of individuals. It is through a Livingstone, a Judson, a Carey, that whole nations have been brought to the feet of Jesus, to sit clothed and in their right mind.

If, therefore, some lone and single-handed Christian worker should read these words, there is no reason for despair. Art thou a cypher? but thou mayest have God in front of thee! Art thou but a narrow strait! yet the whole ocean of Godhead is waiting to pour through thee! The question is not what thou canst or canst not do, but what thou art willing for God to do. When God makes use of one man, he becomes the father of a vast multitude as Abraham of Israel. The only condition is the presence of God in us, with us, through us. Open thy whole being to God; for God is about to comfort the waste places of Zion. He will make her wilderness like Eden, and her desert like the garden of the Lord; joy and gladness shall be found therein, thanksgiving and the voice of melody.

(2) THE IMPERISHABLENESS OF SPIRITUAL QUALITY.—In the following verses there is a marvellous contrast between the material and the un-material, the temporal and the eternal. The gaze of the people is directed to the heavens above and the earth beneath. Those heavens seem stable enough, far removed from the convulsions and shocks of time. To them surely no change can come. Yet they shall vanish like a puff of smoke borne down the wind. And as for the earth, it shall wax old. Nature has often been described as God's vesture, the veil under which He hides. But the day shall come when it shall be laid aside. There shall be new heavens and a new earth, for the first heavens and the first earth shall pass away. But amid the general wreck, spiritual qualities will remain imperishably the same. "My salvation shall be for ever, and my righteousness shall not be abolished" (6).

This shall be for ever true of God. We cannot discern what awaits us in the near future. This world is destined to see—and perhaps soon—the sudden unveiling of the

109

Divine plan, to which God has been working through the ages; vast natural convulsions; nature in the throes of travail; the advent of the King; the setting up of the Judgment; the Resurrection. But though such things take place around us, we need not doubt that God will remain the same—his love and faithfulness, his covenant and promise, his purpose and choice. Our friend's heart is the same when he appears in a new attire; and God will be the same in his feelings and dealings towards us amid the crash of matter and the wreck of worlds as He is to-day. We shall still be his adopted children, still accepted in the Beloved, still included in his everlasting covenant, still one with his Son, as members of his Body and his Bride.

The Jews took great comfort in the thought of God's unchangeableness. Had He not said that his righteousness was near and his salvation gone forth; that his arms should judge the people, and the isles wait for Him? Then Babylon might fall beneath the assault of Cyrus, and the whole world be in confusion; floods of anarchy might burst on the nation, yet God's word would be fulfilled; He could not recede from his purpose or alter it; they might possess their souls in the sure confidence that, as He had promised, so He would perform. Some such assurance may well steal into our hearts, as we anticipate the changes that are always coming over ourselves, our homes, our churches, and our time. Everything else alters—the most stable foundations of our trust give way—but God is unchangeably the same; the qualities of his character are as permanent as his throne.

This shall be for ever true of man. When we partake of God's righteousness, and assimilate it, we acquire a permanence which defies time and change. The love we derive from the heart of God, and have to each other, abideth for ever. The peace we receive deepens in its perennial flow. The patience, courage, strength of character, which we acquire here with so much pain, are not to go out as a candle, nor vanish as a puff of smoke. If it were so, what would become of God's infinite painstaking! No; our school-house may be in ruins, and not a vestige of it left; the primers from which we read, the hard forms on which we sat, may vanish, but the characters we acquired shall outlive the world of matter. These

110

shall be for ever, and shall not be abolished. Oh, let us not murmur at the slow progress of our education, and at the care that God takes for us thoroughly to master each lesson—turning it back, making us review it again and again. He is working for eternity.

What a lesson is given in these words of the relative value of things! To the man of the world the *having* is all-important; to the man of faith the *being*. The child of sense sacrifices all for what is but a puff of smoke, or a moth-eaten garment at the best; but the child of eternity looks for a kingdom that hath foundations, whose Builder and Maker is God—where the moth does not eat, nor rust corrupt, nor fire consume, nor change intrude. A man's life consisteth not in the abundance of the things that he possesses, but in meekness, faith, fidelity, devotion, love.

(3) THE IMPOTENCE OF MAN.—These exiled Jews hardly dared to hope they would be able to break away from their foes. The air was laden with their reproaches and revilings. What mercy could they hope for from those who refused to stint their bitter words? When their oppressors passed from malignant threats to action, there would be little shrift or quarter. We have all known something of this fear of man, who seemed waiting to destroy. But to us, as to the exiles in Babylon, the Divine word comes, "Fear ye not, neither be dismayed" (7).

The paragraph closes with an application of the word used by the great Servant of Himself. "The moth shall eat them up," we heard Him saying to Himself; "they shall all wax old as a garment" (50:9). But now we are bidden to apply those same expressions to ourselves. "The moth shall eat them up like a garment, and the worm shall eat them like wool" (51:8) With these assurances behind us, we may face a world in arms. Men may try to wear out the saints, but they must fail; because our souls are fed from the perennial springs of the Divine nature, and because God has imparted to us both patience and courage which are eternal in their nature. He will take care of his own.

17

"AWAKE, AWAKE!"

"Oh, quickly come, dread Judge of all!
For, awful though Thine advent be,
*   All shadows from the truth will fall,*
And falsehood die, in sight of Thee.
*   Oh quickly come! for doubt and fear*
Like clouds dissolve when Thou art near."

Tuttiett

(Isaiah 52:1)

The thrice "Hearken" of the preceding paragraphs is followed by the thrice "Awake" of these. The first is addressed to the arm of Jehovah, which, with rich poetic licence, is imaged as asleep; the other two to Jerusalem, whether to the ruined city, or to her sons then by "the waters of Babylon" (51:9, 17; 52:1).

Let us take the central paragraph first (51:17). There Jerusalem is addressed as stupefied by some intoxicating potion. She has drained it to its dregs, and lies as one asleep. But her drunkenness is not of wine, nor of strong drink; she has drunk at the hand of the Lord "the cup of his fury." Such imagery is often used by the prophets, of the cup of God's wrath drunk by those on whom it descends and inflicting on them the insensibility and stupefaction with which we are but too familiar as the effect of excessive drinking.

The whole city has succumbed under the spell. Her sons have fainted, and lie strewn in all the streets, like antelopes snared in the hunters' nets, from which their struggles have failed to extricate them. Amid such circumstances, the servant of Jehovah is introduced, crying, "Awake, awake! stand up, O Jerusalem, which hast drunk at the hand of the Lord the cup of his fury."

As the tremor of light in the eastern sky stirs the life of the sleeping city; as the warm breath of the south wind dissipates the snow and frost of winter; as the whisper, "Talitha cumi," aroused the sleeping maiden in the house of Jairus—so did that call awake the stupefied city of Zion, and all suddenly the pulse of life began to throb. Arousing herself, she thought God had been asleep, and called on Him to awake. She had to learn that it was not so. It was she that had been sleeping; and therefore the appeal was flashed back from God to her, "Awake, awake! put on thy strength, O Zion; put on thy beautiful garments, O Jerusalem, the holy city."

There are other soporifics than the wrath of God: the air of the enchanted ground; the laudanum of evil companionship; the drugs of worldly pleasure, of absorption in business, of carnal security. By these we are all liable to be thrown into a deep sleep. The army of the Lord is too apt to put off the armour of light, and resign itself to heavy slumbers, till the clarion voice warns that it is high time to awake. Not once nor twice in the life of the disciples did they become heavy with sleep. And we, too, lose the ardour of our zeal, the warmth of our love, the certainty of our faith, the enthusiasm of our service, and become benumbed and insensible. Merciful Awakener of souls, we adore Thee for so often standing beside us, and saying, "Awake, awake!" Often we have started from slumber, thinking that Thou hadst been asleep, whereas it was ourselves!

(1) ZION'S APPEAL TO GOD.—"Awake, awake! put on strength, O arm of the Lord" (51:9).

The first symptom of awaking is a cry. It is so with a child. Wherever the mother may be engaged about the house, she is on the alert for the first sounds of her babe's awakening. She says, "Did you hear the child cry?" It is so with the soul. When Saul of Tarsus was converted, the heavenly watchers said, "Behold, he prayeth." It is so with the Church. The outpouring of the spirit of prayer is the first symptom of renewal and revival, just as the murmur of the streams in the valleys shows that the snows are melting on the Upper Alps.

The cry in this case was founded in a mistake. The prayer refers to what is familiar to us all in the Divine life. There are ebbs and flows; the winter and summer; the Transfiguration height, and the valley with its demoniac child. Sometimes God seems alert, alive, and energetic;

H   113

the pulse of his energy stirs in us; his voice summons us to new and heroic tasks. At other times a heavy lethargy hangs over the landscape of earth, and intercepts our view of heaven. But our mistake is to attribute the cause to God instead of finding it in ourselves. If there are variations in our inner life, it is because our rate of reception differs from time to time. It is not God who sleeps, but we. It is not for God to awake, but for us. It is not necessary for the Divine arm to gird on strength, but for the human to take that which is within its easy reach.

The cry is short and earnest. Thrice the suppliant cries, "Awake!" When we are suddenly startled from sleep, conscious that something is wrong and needs mending, we cry vigorously to God. This is well, even though we shall learn presently that we are ourselves to blame because there has been a pause, a break in our receptivity. Still, earnestness is good, even though at first it may be in a wrong direction.

The best basis for our cry is memory of the past. "Art thou not it that cut Rahab (*i.e.* Egypt) in pieces, that pierced the dragon?" (*i.e.* of the Nile) (51:9). It is well to quote past experiences as arguments for faith. Our past life will have missed its aim if it has not revealed God to us. Each incident is intended to show us some new trait in his character for us to treasure for all coming time. Not that we expect God to repeat Himself; but that we learn to say, if He did all this, He is resourceful, tender-hearted, wise, and strong: there is no emergency with which He cannot grapple, no need He cannot fulfil. He gave manna—He surely can provide water. He delivered from Egypt—He can certainly emancipate from Babylon. He dried up the waters of the great deep, and made the depths of the sea a way for his ransomed—then surely He can make the wilderness a pool of water, and all the mountains a way.

The arm of God is strong. It stretched forth the heavens and laid the foundation of the earth (51:13). The same energy has left a lasting monument of its might in the works of nature. Surely, child of God, it is able to defend thee; to be thy bulwark and defence; thy fortress against thy mightiest foes. The fury of the oppressor may seem ready to destroy, but it shall break in vain on the arm of God; as the sea breaks on the long harbour wall, which is built out into the angry breakers, and behind which the smallest craft may shelter.

The arm of God is far-reaching. It reaches down into the pit (51:14). There is no depth so profound to which it will not stoop. The psalmist said—"If I make my bed in hell, Thou art there." Like Jonah, we may go down to the bottom of the mountains, compassed with the waters, and wrapped about with weeds; yet thence shall God bring us. "Nor depth ... can separate us from the love of God which is in Jesus Christ our Lord." However low we sink, underneath are the everlasting arms. They are always underneath.

The arm of God is tender. It comforts us (51:12). It is what the arm of the mother is to the sick and tired child; what the arm of love is to the beloved, who leans on it with a sense of happy security! Those arms were stretched out on the cross, spread wide to encompass the world. They welcome to the tenderest bosom that heaves anywhere in the universe. John found it a soft place at the Last Supper. Let us not hesitate to lean back in that embrace and near that heart, to be comforted when our heart is sick and the flesh faints. None can pluck us thence.

> *"Safe in the arms of Jesus,*
> *Safe on his loving breast,*
> *There by his love o'er-shaded*
> *Sweetly my soul shall rest."*

We are too apt to forget all this, to forget the Lord our Maker and Redeemer (51:13). We think more of the earth than of the over-arching heavens; more of the fading grass than of the tree of life; more of man than of God. The near has obscured the distant; the flaring gas-lamps have dimmed the shine of the stars; the human has eclipsed the Divine. Oh, think of Him who sits at the right hand of God, the seat of his resistless and unceasing energy; and believe that He is between thee and all adverse circumstances, though they be ready to destroy. To fear continually all the day because of the fury of the oppressor, is impossible for those who dwell all day

115

between the shoulders of Emmanuel, and are hidden in the shadow of his hand (51:16).

(2) THE APPEAL TO ZION.—When we become thoroughly awake, and have time for reflection, we discover that the fault and blame lie entirely with ourselves. It is not God who has been lethargic: He can neither slumber nor sleep ; we have slept.

It is blessed to be awaked out of sleep. Life is passing by so rapidly ; the radiant glory of the Saviour may be missed unless we are on the alert, or we may fail to give Him the sympathy He needs, and an angel will be summoned to do our work. Besides, the world needs the help of men who give no sleep to their eyes nor slumber to their eyelids, but are always eager to help it in its need. Being awake, we shall discover two sets of attire awaiting us. The first is strength, the other beauty ; and each has its counterpart in the New Testament, the one in Eph. 6, the other in Col. 3. Put on the whole armour of God. Put on the Lord Jesus Christ—his temper, spirit, and character.

We must put on our beautiful garments. There should be a bloom and beauty about us. Not only garments, but *beautiful* garments. The emblem of the life to which we are called is the bridegroom decked with a garland, or the bride with her jewels, or the garden filled with blossom (61:10, 11). We must not only do right things, we must do them beautifully ; not only speak the truth, but speak it in love ; not only give to the poor, but to do it unobtrusively, without the appearance of patronage or ostentation. The beauty of the Lord our God must be upon us. The apostle's enumeration of the clothing of the redeemed soul is largely occupied with its temper and disposition, what might be called its bloom—"compassion, kindness, humility, meekness, long-suffering."

We cannot weave these. We are not able to spin such a cocoon out of our own nature, nor are we required to do so. They are all prepared for us in Jesus ; we have only to put them on, by putting Him on. Assume the meekness, gentleness, and purity of Jesus. Be a partaker of the kingdom and patience which are in Jesus (Rev. 1:9). Or, to state the same truth in a different way, take Jesus to be what God has made Him—wisdom, righteousness, sanctification, and redemption.

116

This can only be done when the heart is at leisure. There must be deep recollection of soul in the Master's presence ; then the reverent and glad attiring of the soul with the qualities of his glorious nature, and the reckoning that they are assumed in response to the act of faith. The beautiful garments await the poorest, weakest, unlikeliest. None of God's own need go in rags ; none need be arrayed in anything else than the light with which God is said to cover Himself. "Thou coverest Thyself with light, as with a garment." "Let us put off the works of darkness, and put on the armour of light."

We must put on strength. "Put on thy strength, O Zion." God provides strength for every possible emergency or demand in life. Whatever call is made upon us, there is always a sufficiency of grace by which it may be met. Undoubtedly, temptation and trial are permitted to come so that we may be compelled to appropriate supplies which lie within our reach, but of which we should not have availed ourselves, unless hard pressed and put to it. Always the danger is that, even under such circumstances we should fail to put on the strength which is stored for us in Jesus Christ our Lord.

We are not bidden to purchase strength, or generate it by our resolutions, prayers, and agonisings ; *but to put it on.* It is already prepared, and only awaits appropriation. Put on thy strength, O tempted one! Before passing from the quiet morning hour into the arena which has so often witnessed failure and defeat, put on the might of the risen Saviour. Do not simply pray to be kept, or to be helped, but arm thyself with the whole armour of God ; take hold of his strength and be at peace ; wrap thyself about with the mail of Him who is stronger than the strong man armed. Reckon that it is thine. Dare to believe that thou art more than a match for thy worst foes. Say with David, "I will not be afraid of ten thousands of people who set themselves round about. The Lord is my light and my salvation, whom shall I fear? the Lord is the strength of my life, of whom shall I be afraid?"

We must expect to be delivered from the dominion of sin. Babylon had been bidden to descend from her throne and sit in the dust ; Jerusalem is commanded to arise from the dust and sit on her throne. The bands of

117

her neck were to be unloosed, her gates were never again to be passed by the uncircumcised and the unclean. So entire was to be the deliverance of Jehovah, that she was henceforth to be "the holy city," separate for the exclusive service of God.

These words have an application for us. The inner citadel of the heart is intended to be God's alone. He purchased the site ; He built and reared its walls ; He claims it as the seat of the royal residence. The heart is the Holy See. And if we are thoroughly yielded to Him as our Judge, our Lawgiver, and our King, He will save us. The walls shall be salvation, and the gates praise. There shall not enter the abominable, the unclean, nor the lying thought. Diabolus shall be driven from Mansoul, and Emmanuel shall be enthroned in His glory and beauty. Then the bells shall ring, and the streets shall be filled with chorister-bands, and white-robed priests, and shining ones with harps and vials full of odours.

18

"DEPART YE, DEPART YE!"

"Break up the heavens, O Lord! and far
Thro' all yon starlight keen,
Draw me, thy bride—a glittering star
In raiment white and clean!"

Tennyson

(Isaiah 52: 7-12)

At last the climax of the long prophetic stairway is gained. The prophet had anticipated it in a previous passage (49:20), but had been diverted by the objections urged against the possibility of such an issue of the long captivity. It could not be, Israel argued. It was unheard of, that a strong nation like Babylon should let one of its captive peoples go free without fee or reward. The archives of all nations might be searched in vain for such a precedent. One by one, the servant of God had met and answered these objections ; had declared his own unalterable resolve ; had startled their lethargy with the thrice "Hearken!" and the thrice "Awake!" And now again he puts the trumpet to his lips, and announces the Exodus—"Depart ye, depart ye! go ye out from thence, touch no unclean thing."

From the glowing periods of this paragraph we can reconstruct the picture of the return from exile, as it presented itself to the seer. It was notably the return of the Lord to Zion (8, R.V.). The stately procession moves slowly and fearlessly. It is not the escape of a band of fugitive slaves, dreading pursuit and recapture: "Ye shall not go out in haste, neither shall ye go by flight." Before it speed the messengers, appearing on the sky-line of the mountains of Zion, with good tidings of good, publishing peace, and publishing salvation (7).

The main body is composed of white-robed priests, bearing with reverent care the holy vessels, which Nebuchadnezzar carried from the temple, which Belshazzar introduced with mockery into his feast, but which Cyrus restored. Their number and weight are carefully specified, 5,400 in all (Ezra 1 : 7–11).

As the procession emerges from its four months of wilderness march on the mountains which were about Jerusalem, her watchmen, who had long waited for the happy moment, lift up their voice ; with the voice together do they sing. They see eye to eye. And the waste places of Jerusalem, with their charred wood and scorched stones, break forth into joy and sing together. The valleys and hills become vocal, constituting an orchestra of praise ; and the nations of the world are depicted as coming to behold, and acknowledge that the Lord had made bare his holy arm. But they do not see —what is hidden from all but anointed eyes—that the Lord goes before his people, and comes behind as their rearward ; so that their difficulties are surmounted by Him before they reach them, and no foe can attack them from behind.

The literal fulfilment of this splendid prevision is described in the Book of Ezra. There we find the story of the return of a little band of Jews, 1.700 only in number. They halted at the River Ahava, the last station before they entered the desert, for three days, to put themselves with fasting and prayer into God's hand. They had no experience of desert marching. Their caravan was rendered unwieldly by the number of women and children in it. They had to thread a district infested by wild bands of robbers. But they scorned to ask for an escort of soldiers and horsemen to protect them, so sure were they that their God went before them to open up the way, and came behind to defend against attack. In the midst of the march were priests and Levites, with their sacred charge of which Ezra had said, "Watch and keep them, until ye weigh them in the chambers of the house of the Lord."

We do not read of the songs of the pilgrim-host, as here foreshadowed. But they may have risen morning and evening on the desert air, enlivening the monotony of the march. There are many psalms which date from this period; and these may have been favourites with the pilgrim-host, as they passed over the dunes of the desert or sat around the camp-fires. In several respects there seems a falling short between the radiant expectation of the prophet, and the actual accomplishment in the story of Ezra: but we must remember that it is the business of the historian to record the facts, rather than the emotions that coloured them, as the warm colours of the sun colour the hard grey rocks. And is it not always so, that through our want of faith and obedience we come short of the fullness of blessing which our God has prepared for us?

We may learn some of those qualities which should characterise us in our march through this desert world to the city of God.

(1) THERE SHOULD BE PERPETUAL EXODUS.—The Jews had become habituated to Babylon. Custom makes most things endurable. In the days of Ezra, few were left who remembered the anguish of the captivity. The people, born in the land of their conquerors, had conformed their methods of life to the conditions of that great civilisation, which was destined to exert an influence upon them in all after-days. Some of them probably longed for the expiry of the allotted years of captivity. But the majority were settled in comfortable, and in some cases opulent, circumstances, and not at all anxious to exchange Babylon for the ruins of Zion. The result was, that they became dispersed throughout the Orient, building syna-

gogues, enjoying material prosperity; but becoming lost as a river in the sand.

In all lives there are Babylons, which have no claim on the redeemed of Jehovah. We may have entered them, not without qualms of conscience; but, as time has passed, our reluctance has been overcome. A comradeship has grown up between us and one from whose language and ways we once shrank in horror. An amusement now fascinates us, which we regarded with suspicion and conscientious scruple. A habit of life dominates us from which we once shrank as from infection. A method of winning money now engrosses us; but we can well remember how difficult it was to coax conscience to engage in it. These are Babylons, which cast their fatal spell over the soul, and against which the voice of God urgently protests. "Depart ye, depart ye! go ye out from thence."

When stepping out from Babylon to an unwonted freedom, we naturally shrink back before the desert march, the sandy wastes, the ruined remnants of happier days. Those who remembered the first temple, wept when the foundations of the second were laid; and Nehemiah could not restrain his tears at the sight of the heaps of rubbish. But we shall receive more than we renounce. Forsaking the outward and temporal, we shall find ourselves possessed of the inner and eternal. In the desert we see the eternal constellations burning above us; we feel the breath of God upon our faces; we have a reward which would compensate for a hundred such renunciations: "I will receive you, and be a Father unto you."

(2) IT SHOULD BE WITHOUT HASTE.—"Ye shall not go out in haste." There are many English proverbs which sum up the observation of former days and tell how foolish it is to be in a hurry. But, outside of God, there is small chance of obeying these wise maxims. The age is so feverish. Men haste to be rich; they rush from pleasure to pleasure; they make the tour of the world in six months; they do Rome in a week. We cram children's minds with undigested knowledge. And this feverish, unresting spirit has invaded our religious life, our closets, our musings, our worship. It is impossible to give ourselves thoroughly to anything, because our watch is always in our hand lest we miss our train.

121

No great picture was ever painted in a hurry. No great book was ever written against time. No great discovery was ever granted to the student who could not watch in Nature's antechamber for the gentle opening of her door. The greatest naturalist of our time devoted eight whole years almost entirely to barnacles. Well might John Foster long for the power of touching mankind with the spell of *"Be quiet, be quiet."*

In this our Lord is our best exemplar. He moved slowly and deliberately through his crowded years. He had leisure for every appeal, for the touch of each wan hand. There was no trace of feverishness or unrest. Men were always urging Him onward ; but he answered, "Your time is always ready ; mine is not yet." His secret, using our human phrase, lay in his simple faith. He believed, and therefore did not make haste. Every incident in his life had been arranged by his Father's unfailing care. There was time for everything, and everything must be fitted to its time. If there were work to be done, He was secure against arrest till it was finished. Herod could not kill Him till He was perfected.

This hastelessness was possible to Israel so long as the people believed that God was ordering, preceding, and followed their march. Why should they go by flight, as though the foe were about to fall on the hindmost, when God was their rearward! Why rush forward to gain some advantage, if God went in front to seek out their resting-place! When we really believe in God, his providence, and his arrangement of our lives, to us too there will come this blessed calm ; and whenever we are tempted to get feverish and fretful, we shall compel ourselves to go out beneath the arch of God's eternal years, saying, "Return, my soul, unto thy rest. God is behind, intercepting pursuit from past failure and sin."

(3) WE MUST BE AT PEACE ABOUT THE WAY.—In early life our path seems clearly defined. We must follow the steps of others, depend on their maxims, act on their advice ; till suddenly we find ourselves at the head of the march ; no footprints before us on the expanse of moorland, or of sand. It is only when the years grow upon us that this sense of *waylessness*, as it has been termed, oppresses us. So the exiles must have felt when they left Ahava and started on the desert march.

At such times the lips of Christ answer, "I am the Way." Throughout the Acts of the Apostles, we find that the almost invariable term by which the Gospel was known was "the Way"; as if those first believers were intoxicated with the rapture of feeling that at last they had discovered the track of the blessed life, the pathway which would thread the perplexities of earth, and bring them to the city of God. And if we had asked any one of them to give an equivalent for the term they so constantly employed, they would have answered, without a moment's hesitation, JESUS. Probably there is no better way of ascertaining the true method of life, than by asking ourselves how Jesus would have acted under similar circumstances. His temper, his way of looking at things, his will, resolves all perplexities.

All this was set forth in the figure before us. "The Lord will go before you." When the people came out of Egypt, Jehovah preceded the march in the Shekinah cloud that moved softly above the ark. When it advanced, they struck their tents and followed; when it brooded, they halted and fixed the camp. It was the one visible and unerring guide through those trackless wastes. There was nothing of this sort when Ezra led the first detachment of exiles to Zion; but, though unseen, the Divine leader was equally in the forefront of the march. Thus it is also in daily experience. When the way forks, when the track dies in the grass, when the expanse of desert lies in front without a beaten pathway—stand still; take an observation; hush all voices in the presence of Christ; ask what He would have done; ask what He would wish you to do. Remember that the Good Shepherd, when He puts forth his sheep, goes before them, and they follow Him. Jesus is ever going before us in every call to duty, every prompting to self-sacrifice, every summons to comfort, help, and save. With God behind as Rearguard, and God in front as Leader, and God encompassing us with songs of deliverance, there can be no doubt that we shall at last reach that Zion in which there are no waste places, and whose walls have never reeled before the shock of armed men.

(4) WE MUST BE PURE.—"Touch no unclean thing. Be ye clean, ye that bear the vessels of the Lord." Those vessels, as we have seen, were very precious. The enum-

123

eration is made with minute accuracy (Ezra 8:26). But they were above all things holy unto the Lord. For generations they had been employed in temple service. Those that bore them were no common men ; but Levites specially summoned to the work, and possessed at least of a ceremonial cleanliness. Thus they passed across the desert, holy men bearing the holy vessels.

Through this world, unseen by mortal eye, a procession is passing, threading its way across continents of time. It bears holy vessels. The forms of expression in which Divine truth is enshrined may be compared to the vessels of the old dispensation, set apart to serve the purposes of the sanctuary. Testimony to God's truth, the affirmation of things unseen and eternal, the announcement of the facts of redemption—such are our sacred charge. We must contend earnestly for the faith once delivered to the saints. Take heed to thyself, and *to the doctrine*. The greatest service the Church can give to the world is its perpetual witness to the truth of God's being ; to the facts of redemption, of judgment, and of the world to come. Concerning all these, the olden charge is given us, "Watch ye and keep them, until ye weigh them before the chiefs of the priests and of the Levites, in the chambers of the house of the Lord."

What manner of persons ought we not to be, to whom so high a ministry is entrusted! How careful that our holy trust should not be forfeited because of our unholy life! How eager lest the glistening glory of our charge be blurred or dimmed by our thumbmarks! How watchful that the testimony of a doctrine be not traversed by the life of those that profess it! Men estimate the worth of the truths to which we bear witness by the worth of our personal character. Let us commend the Gospel by the holiness and elevation of our lives.

Before that procession we are told that waste places would break forth into song. It is a fair conception, as though their feet changed the aspect of the territories through which they passed. What was desert when they came to it, was paradise as they left it! What were ruins, became walls! Where there had been hostility, suspicion, and misunderstanding, there came concord and peace, the watchmen seeing eye to eye.

This is a true portraiture of the influence of the religion of Jesus over the hearts and lives of men. Creation

124

herself, which now groans and travails, shall presently burst into hallelujahs like those with which the Psalter closes. God give us grace to join in that procession, and with beautiful array pass onward without haste, under Divine convoy, till the glowing predictions of prophecy and psalm be realised in an emancipated universe!

But let us never forget the importance of prayer, as a necessary link in the achieving of these marvels. In the former chapter, there had been one eager and intense petition, "Awake, awake, put on strength, O arm of the Lord. Awake as in the ancient days!" That prayer had entered into the ear of the Lord God of Sabaoth, and here we are told that "the Lord hath made bare his holy arm in the eyes of all the nations." Pray on, O child of God! thy breath is not mis-spent; thy tears are not wasted; "Behold, the Lord God will come as a mighty one, and his arm shall rule for Him."

19

THE VINDICATION OF CHRIST

"It is the Day;
No more sad watchings by the midnight sea,
No twilight gray,
But, crowned with light and immortality,
He stands from henceforth, triumphing alway
In God's own Day."

B. M.

(Isaiah 52:13-15)

There is only one brow which this crown of thorns will fit. As the eunuch sat in his chariot and read this wonderful lyric of sorrow even unto death, which in its rhythm and diction stands alone amongst these marvellous chapters, he questioned of whom the writer spake. "I pray thee," he said to Philip, "of whom speaketh the prophet thus? of himself, or of some other?" The evangelist, in reply, commenced to preach from this same scripture, Jesus.

125

Jesus is the Key which the whole New Testament, in many allusions, puts into our hands to unlock these mysteries, in which heaven and earth, the eternal and the temporal, the love of God and the weakness of man blend, with no apparent horizon line. But even apart from this precise testimony of the Holy Ghost, we could have found none worthy to take this scroll and open it seal by seal, but the Lamb in the midst of the throne, the Lion of the tribe of Judah, the Son of God Himself.

Efforts have been made to apply this or the other line and fragment of this prophecy to one and another of the great sufferers of history: to Jeremiah, to Ezekiel, to some unknown martyr in the days of the captivity! and it is quite likely, since sorrow and pain are the heritage of all, that in some particulars this vision was realised by lesser men than the Son of Man. A child's hand may strike notes on the Freyburg organ! But who of woman born, but the Christ, could take these words in their entirety and say?—"I claim that all this was realised in myself ; this portraiture is mine ; there is neither line nor lineament here which has not its correspondence in me." Should any of the sons of men put in such a claim, he would encounter at once the full force of a world's ridicule and contempt. But when the Man of Nazareth approaches, and claims to have fulfilled this dark and bitter record ; when He opens his heart and shows its scars ; when He enumerates his unknown sufferings, and asks if there were ever grief like his—no one dares to challenge his right to claim and annex this empire as his own ; nay, deep down in the heart, there is a tacit confession that probably He touched yet profounder depths, and drank more bitter draughts, than even these words record.

This elegy of sorrow is unfortunately divided by the arbitrary arrangement of the chapters in our Bibles. Really, it begins at 52: 13, with the word which so often arrests attention in this Book, "Behold." It consists of five stanzas of three verses each, the closing paragraphs being somewhat longer. No English translation can give a conception of the cadence and sad minor tones which sob through its chords.

The theme is the sufferings of the Servant of God ; the wrong conclusions which his fellows formed of them ; and the triumphant vindication which He has received.

(1) A STORY OF SORROW AND PAIN.—Three mysteries meet here; as clouds brood darkly over the mountains when a thunder-storm is imminent.

The mystery of humiliation. The tender plant; the sucker painfully pushing its way through the crust of the caked ground; the absence of natural attractiveness. Such imagery awaits and receives its full interpretation from the New Testament, with its story of Christ's peasant parentage, his manger-bed, and lowly circumstances—fisherfolk his choice disciples; poverty his constant lot; the common people his devoted admirers; thieves and malefactors on either side of his cross; the lowly and poor the constituents of his Church. This were humiliation indeed, though the irregularities of human lot are scarce distinguishable from the heights whence He came. The profoundest stoop of his humility was that He became man at all. He was Infinite in his unstinted blessedness; rich with the wealth that has flowered out into the universe; radiant in the dazzling beauty of perfect moral excellence. What agony, therefore, must have been his to breathe our tainted air, to live in daily contact with sinners, and to be perpetually surrounded by the most miserable and plague-stricken of the race! And that He should die! That the Life-Giver should pass under the dark portal of the grave! That the Son of God should become obedient to a death of ignominy and shame at the hands of men! This is a mystery of humiliation indeed.

The mystery of sorrow. You can see its ineffaceable mintmark on that marred face. We need no further proof that He was a Man of Sorrows, and acquainted with grief. But what is sorrow? Each of us knows by experience what it is; but who can define it, or say in a sentence of what it consists? It is that emotion which results when love meets with dark shadows threatening its beloved. There is doubtless a selfish kind of sorrow which repines at losses that can be counted in gold, and bewails the curtailing of sensual gratification. But this may not be mentioned here, where we are within the precincts of the sorrow of the world's Redeemer. We are treating sorrow as it might exist in his peerless heart, and in those who are being moulded in his image.

Such are capable of a Divine love; and by the very

127

measure of that capacity they are liable to supreme sorrow. When love beholds its objects eluding its embrace —their love turning cold, their souls poisoned by misunderstanding and misrepresentation, their lives engulfed by eddies from which it would save them if it could, but they refuse its aid—then there is sorrow; as rain meeting a blast of frosty air will turn to snow, and fall in white flakes.

We need go no further for the reason why Jesus sorrowed as He did. It could not have been otherwise. Men could not be loved by Him without causing Him infinite pain. Hast thou not wounded Him, crucified Him, wrung his heart, just because thou wert not able to appreciate the delicacy and sensitiveness of the heart which was pouring out its stores for thee with prodigal lavishness? Throughout the ages He has come to his own, and they have barred the door to his entrance; He has desired to gather them, as a hen her chicks, but they have refused Him; He has come into his garden to gather the precious fruit and spices that would refresh his soul, but He has found the wall in ruins, and the choice stores rifled; slights, where there should have been tenderness; rebuffs, where He looked for a welcome; put to open shame, instead of in the inner shrine of esteem and love. Surely this will account for this mystery of sorrow.

The mystery of pain. Wounded, bruised, chastised; the spittle of the soldiery on his face; the scourge ploughing long red seams in his flesh; the bloody sweat beading his brow; the cry "Forsaken!". There is suffering here! Well might Pilate cry, as though to move the pity of the crowd with such a spectacle of misery, "Behold the Man!"

A suggestion of the anguish which our blessed Lord endured, and which the liturgy of the Greek church refers to as "his unknown sufferings," is given in those remarkable words of the Epistle to the Hebrews, which tell us that after pouring out his prayers and supplications with strong crying and tears unto Him who was able to save Him from death, He was heard in that he feared. In every age Christian men have pondered those words, asking what they meant. Is it not at least possible for Jesus to have meant that He was so wrung with anguish, that He thought He must die in the garden before ever He reached his cross? The pressure of pain was almost unendurable; and there was every fear that his nature would collapse ere the expiatory sacrifice could be offered. If this is the right rendering of the passage, what a marvellous conception is afforded of the sea-billows of suffering which surged up and rolled over the human nature of the Redeemer! If the anticipation of Calvary so wrung his heart, what must not the endurance have been! Such was the mystery of pain.

O King of suffering and sorrow! Monarch of the marred face, none has ever approached Thee in the extremity of Thy grief; we bow the knee, and bid thee "All Hail!" We are conquered by Thy tears and woes; our hearts are enthralled; our souls inspired; our lives surrendered to Thy disposal for the execution of purposes which cost Thee so dear.

(2) WRONG SUPERFICIAL CONCLUSIONS.—Every age has connected misery with guilt, anguish with iniquity, suffering with sin. Special pain has been regarded as the indication of special wrong-doing. It was in vain that Job protested his innocence; his friends insisted that the reason of his awful sufferings must be sought in evils, which, though he had screened them from the gaze of men, were doubtless well known to himself and God. The awful absence of sight which the blind man had suffered from his birth made the disciples speculate as to whether he or his parents had perpetrated some terrible crime, of which that privation was the evidence and the result. And when, on the storm-swept shore of Malta, the apostle's hand was suddenly encircled by the viper, creeping out of the heat, the natives concluded that he was a murderer, who, though he had escaped the sea, could not escape the penalty which justice demanded. So the verdict which the thoughtless crowd might be disposed to pass on the unique sufferings of Christ would be that they were, without doubt, richly merited. This, in point of fact, is the explanation put into the mouth of his own people by the prophet: "We did esteem Him, smitten of God, and afflicted."—

Perhaps the members of the Pharisee party who consented to his death, swept on against their better judgment by the virulence of Caiaphas and Annas, may have comforted themselves, as the shadows of that memorable day fell on the empty crosses, that such sufferings could not have been permitted by God to overtake the Nazarene had He not been guilty of the blasphemy for which He was adjudged worthy of death.

But all this while Jesus opened not his mouth. Silent before Caiaphas, except when his refusal to speak might appear to compromise his claims to death ; silent before Herod, as one to whom speech was vain ; silent before Pilate, except when the Roman governor seemed really eager to know the truth—"He was led as a lamb to the slaughter, and as a sheep, dumb before her shearers, so He opened not his mouth."

Why this speechlessness? In part it was due to the Saviour's clear apprehension of the futility of arguing with those who were bent on crucifying Him. It was also due to the quiet rest of his soul on God, as He committed Himself to Him that judgeth righteously, and anticipated the hour when the Father would arise to give Him a complete vindication. But it was due also to his consciousness of carrying in his breast a golden secret, another explanation of his sufferings than men were aware of, a Divine solution of the mystery of human guilt.

We give our highest eulogy to those who suffer for others without a murmur of complaint ; carrying silently a load of pain and grief which these have caused them ; misunderstood and maligned, but keeping their lips fast sealed, lest the true reason should escape until the best moment had come for its revelation ; for such strength of purpose we reserve our highest praise. With what reverence then should we not regard the Lord's reticence. He knew the secret that underlay the Levitical dispensation, and that gave all its meaning to his own approaching death—the great law of the transference of suffering. He realised that He was God's Lamb, on whom the sin of the world was lying ; the scapegoat carrying guilt into a land of forgetfulness ; the antitype of bull, and calf, and dove. His soul was quieted under the conviction of these sublime conceptions, and He could afford to be dumb until He had put away sin by the sacrifice of Himself. What though men judged Him falsely, God the Father knew all that was in his heart. Time would vindicate Him presently: what He carried as a secret in his heart would be proclaimed from the housetops of the world.

We all need to learn this lesson. We are so quick to pour the story of our wrongs into the ears of men, complaining of every injury and slight. We are prone to rush into speech or print, justifying our conduct, rebutting false accusations, and demanding justice. All this is unworthy of those who know that God is waiting in the shadow, "keeping watch upon his own," and sure to bring their righteousness to the light, their judgment to the noonday. For the sake of the wrong-doer we should endeavour to arrest the commission of wrong; as Jesus did when He remonstrated with the high priest for his flagrant violation of the principles of Jewish jurisprudence. But where high-handed evil rushes forward, as a wild beast crashes through the slight resistance of osier-beds to reach his prey, then our wisest and most Christ-like attitude is not to revile again, nor threaten, but to lift up our eyes to the hills from whence our help comes.

(3) THE SUFFERER'S VINDICATION.—It may tarry, but it surely comes at length. It came, and is always coming, to Christ. Each age has only established more completely his absolute moral beauty; the dignity and majesty of his bearing under the sufferings of his last hour; and the infinite value of his cross and passion.

Vindicated by the growing convictions of men. We, the prophet says, speaking of men generally—*we* esteemed Him not, because we thought that God was punishing Him for his sin, but now we have discovered that He bore *our* griefs, and carried *our* sorrows; that He was wounded for *our* transgressions, bruised for *our* iniquities, chastened for *our* peace. In other words, the great truth of substitution is looming ever clearer on the conscience and heart of man. As never before, light is breaking on the heights of the doctrine of vicarious suffering, bringing into distinctness that wondrous line of virgin peaks which no human foot but One has ever scaled. Not that we can fully measure or define what Jesus did for us on the cross; but that we are coming to understand that his sufferings there have secured redemption for mankind, and laid the foundation of a temple whose walls are salvation and its gates praise,

131

The growing conviction of this fact is, in part, Christ's vindication.

Vindicated by the trust of each individual soul. Each time one comes to Him, and finds healing, peace, and salvation in his wounds, cleansing in his precious blood, shelter beneath the outspread arms of his cross, He sees his seed, He sees of the travail of his soul, and is satisfied; He is vindicated, and recompensed for all his pain.

Vindicated by his exaltation to the right hand of power. "Ye denied the Holy and Righteous One, and killed the Prince of Life, whom God raised from the dead." That is his vindication, that He is seated on his Father's throne, entrusted with all authority, and able to save to the uttermost all who come. Every cry of angel or seraph that He is worthy; every note of adoration, and tribute from orders of being to us unknown; every crown cast at his feet, or palm waved in his train; every accession of honour and glory as the ages roll; his raising of the dead; his session on the great white throne; his eternal reign— attest the vindication of his Father. "He shall divide a portion with the great, and a spoil with the strong."

> *"Heaven is comforted,—*
> *For that strange warfare is accomplished now,*
> *Her King returned with joy."*

20

FAITH AS A SWITCH

"If thou couldst trust, poor soul,
In Him who rules the whole,
Thou wouldst find peace and rest.
Wisdom and sight are well; but Trust is best."

A. Procter

(Isaiah 53:1 ; John 11:40)

A lawyer whom I know took me the other day to see
the fire-proof strong-room in which he keeps valuable
deeds and securities. It is excavated under the street, and
a passage leads far into the interior, lined on either side
with receptacles for the precious documents. On entering,
he took up what appeared to be a candle, with a cord
attached to it ; the other end he deftly fastened to a switch
at the entrance, by means of which the electricity which
was waiting there poured up the wire hidden in the cord,
glowed at the wick of the china-candle, and we were
able to pass to the end of the passage, uncoiling cord
and wire as we went. That unlighted candle resembles
the Christian worker, apart from the power of the Holy
Ghost. Faith may be compared to the switch by means
of which the saving might of God pours into our life and
ministry.

It cannot be too strongly insisted on, that our faith is
the absolute condition and measure of the exertion of
God's saving might. No faith, no blessing ; little faith,
little blessing ; great faith, great blessing. According to
our faith, so it is always done to us. The saving might of
God's glorious arm may be waiting close against us ;
but it is inoperative unless we are united to it by faith.

The negative and positive sides of this great and important truth are presented in the texts before us: one
of which complains that the arm of God is not revealed,
because men have not believed the inspired report ; the
other affirms from the lips of the Master, that those who

believe shall see the glory of God. The texts between them will help us to understand why some, who are best equipped for service, fail; while others, with very indifferent equipment, achieve great and lasting success.

(1) THE ARM OF GOD.—This expression is often used in the older Scriptures, and everywhere signifies the active, saving energy of the Most High. We first meet with it in his own address to Moses: "I will redeem them with a stretched-out arm." Then, in the triumphal shout that broke from two million glad voices beside the Red Sea —and frequently in the book of Deuteronomy,—we read of the stretched-out arm of Jehovah. It is a favourite phrase with the poets and prophets of Israel—the arm that redeems; the holy arm; the glorious arm; the bared arm of God. We have already noticed how it is bidden awake, and put on strength. This metaphor is somewhat different. The conception is that, owing to the unbelief of Israel, it lies inoperative, hidden under the heavy folds of Oriental drapery; whereas it might be revealed, raising itself aloft in vigorous and effective effort.

All that concerns us now is the relation between faith and the forth-putting of God's saving might. God's arm was revealed at the Red Sea, making a path through its depths by which his ransomed might pass over. Then Moses' faith was in eager and triumphant exercise, and the people believed the report which he had given of the words of Jehovah. But it sank into repose during the long forty years of wandering, because Israel believed not his word.

God's arm was revealed at the Jordan, and through the remarkable career of Joshua; it cleft the river at flood, overthrew the walls of Jericho, chased in flight the armies of the aliens, restrained the deepening shadows of the night, and gave the Land of Promise to the chosen race; and this, because Joshua never wavered in his strong, heroic confidence. But again it sank paralysed and powerless to rest, when, in the days of the judges, the people ceased to exercise the faith to which nothing was impossible. Whenever the fire gleamed up from the dull, white ash, as in the days of Gideon, Barak, Jephthah, and Samson, instantly the arm of the Lord was made bare.

The arm of the Lord was revealed in the days when David's faith realised that the living Lord was still amongst his people, well able to save without mail, or spear, or shield. What a springtide was that! The birds of holy song warbled sweetly under a clear heaven of love; the flowerets of nobility, righteousness, and truth jewelled the soil: the light was that of a morning without clouds. There was no standing against the onset of the soldiers, who in the cave of Adullam, had acquired lessons of heroic faith as well as those of knightly chivalry. But again the arm of God relapsed into quiescence, and allowed the foes of his people to work their will even to their captivity, because Israel's faith had become like the Temple of Solomon, a desecrated and ruined shrine.

As we are taught in the Epistle to the Hebrews, all the great exploits and episodes of Hebrew story were due to the faith which believed that God is a present force in history, and a Rewarder of those who diligently seek Him.

(2) THE LIFE OF THE SON OF MAN.—As this chapter suggests, it seemed, from many points of view, a failure. The arm of the Lord was in Him, though hidden from all save the handful who believed. Probably our Lord never wrought a miracle, unless faith was in exercise on the part either of the recipients or spectators of his saving help. The centurion, though a Gentile; the Syrophœnician woman, though accounted a dog; the leper, though an outcast pariah—drew from Him virtue that healed and saved; whilst the bulk of the nation, and especially the companions of his early life, missed the benediction, which had come so nigh them, because they enwrapt themselves in proud indifference. Through unbelief the branches were deprived of the richness of the Root of David. And the condition of Israel in the world to-day is due to persistent unbelief, which has cut them off from the help of the right arm of the Lord.

(3) A SPECIMEN CASE.—For two days Christ had lingered beyond the Jordan, though urgently needed in Bethany, where life was ebbing fast, and tears were flowing which were not wholly due to the sickness and death of him whom Jesus loved. A sense of forlornness; an inability to account for the delayed advent of the dearest Friend,

who neither came nor sent word—made those tears more bitter. The Master, however, was keenly sensitive to all that was taking place. He knew that sickness had become death, and said presently, "Our friend Lazarus sleepeth." That interval of silence and absence seems to have been filled with prayer; to which He referred in the words He spoke aloud at the grave, that the people might be led to attribute all the glory to his Father, and to appreciate the love and beauty of his character. Before our Lord left his hiding-place He knew that the Father had granted Him, in his human nature, the life of his friend. "I go," said he, "to awake him out of sleep. I was glad that I was not there to stay the fall of life's ebbing tide; because, in raising him from the dead, such a proof will be furnished of my oneness with Jehovah, as to compel your faith, and be a comfort and inspiration in all after days."

But even though our Lord went to Bethany with the assurance that the arm of the Lord would certainly be made bare, yet He must of necessity have the co-operation and sympathy of someone's faith.

Such faith He discovered in Martha. This is startling, and helpful. We should not have been surprised to learn that it was found in Mary; because her still and spiritual nature was so closely akin to his own—she had drunk so deeply into his words; she was capable of such a white-heat of love, consecration, and self-forgetting devotion. But we should not have expected Martha to manifest faith, to connect the stored life of Jesus with the charnel-house where Lazarus lay, four days dead. Yet so it befell. She met Jesus with the assurance that He possessed power enough to have averted death, had He only been in time; she declared her belief that his prayer could secure its will from God, and confessed that for long, in her secret soul, she had believed that Jesus was the Messiah, the Son of God, the long-expected Redeemer. These admissions on her part showed that faith was already within her soul, as a grain of mustard-seed, awaiting the summertide of God's presence, the education of his grace.

There are many earnest Christians, whose energies are taxed to the uttermost by their ministry to others. Philanthropists, housewives, workers in every department of Christian service—such are their engagements that they

136

have no time to sit quietly at the feet of Christ, or mature great schemes of loving sympathy with his plans, as Mary did when she prepared her anointing-oil for her Lord's burial. And yet they are capable of a great faith. Beneath the bustle and rush of life, the impulses of the Divine are being responded to: faith in the living Saviour is ripening to a golden harvest; forces are being generated which will surprise themselves and others. Christ will one day discover, reveal, and educate that faith to great exploits.

He put a promise before her. "Thy brother shall rise again." Faith feeds on promises, as the spark that trembles on the hearth grows by the fuel heaped on and around it. If we consider circumstances, we stagger and faint. But if we look away to the strong clear words of God, and through them to the Promiser, we become, like Abraham, strong in faith, and sure that what God has promised He is able also to perform. Make much of God's Word: faith cometh by hearing. Listen to the report—it will induce belief, and this will secure the revelation of the Almighty arm.

He showed that its fulfilment might be expected here and now. Martha was quite prepared to believe that Lazarus would rise again at the last day; but she had no faith in the immediate vivification of the body that lay in its niche behind the stone. Jesus said "I AM the Resurrection and the Life. Here and now is the power which, on that day of which you speak, shall awaken the dead; do but believe, and you shall see that resurrection anticipated."

Ponder the force of this I AM. It is the present tense of the Eternal. At the burning bush, it was the first lesson that Moses had to learn. God is the I AM. He is; He is here; He is able and willing to do now all that He ever will do in the days that are yet to be. Man is so apt to postpone the miraculous and Divine, till some dim horizon-line has been attained and passed. God has blessed, and He will bless. God did marvels at the first Advent, and He will repeat them at the second. But the present is the period of Divine absenteeism—so we think. Oh to believe that Jesus is waiting to be all that He has ever been to souls, or will be! Oh to hear Him say, "I am

137

Resurrection to the dead: I am the more abundant Life to all who live and believe in Me"!

He aroused her expectancy. For what other reason did He ask that the stone might be rolled away? It is certain that it would have been perfectly easy for his voice to reach the ear of the dead through the stony doorway; and had he willed it, Lazarus could have emerged from the grave, though the stone still sealed its mouth. Almost certainly the direction to remove the stone was intended to awaken Martha's expectation and hope that the arm of the Lord would presently be revealed. And it had the desired result. With quickened eagerness she endeavoured to arrest obedience to his mandate; and when the Lord persisted, and reminded her that this was the opportunity for her faith, her soul leaped up to receive with ardour the blessing He was there to give. She believed, and she beheld the glory of God in the face of Jesus Christ.

The one aim for each of us should be to bring Christ and the dead Lazarus together. Death can no more exist when He is present, than night when the sun is rising. Corruption, impurity, sin, flee before Him to whom the Father gave to have life in Himself, and who came that we might have life, and have it more abundantly. Let your faith make an inlet for the Life-giver into your circle of society, your church, your class, your home. Nothing will suffice if this is lacking. Eloquence, learning, position, these will fail. But faith, though it be of the weakest, simplest nature, will link the Saviour, who is alive for evermore, and has the keys of death and Hades, with those who have been in the graves of sin so long that corruption has asserted its foul dominion over every part of their nature.

Let us ask Christ, our Saviour, to work such faith in us; to develop it by every method of education and discipline; to mature it by his nurturing Spirit, until the arm of God is revealed in us and through us, and the glory of God is manifested before the gaze of men.

At the same time, it is not well to concentrate our thought too much on *faith,* lest we hinder its growth. Look away from faith to the object of faith, and faith will spring of itself. It is the bloom of the soul's health. See to it that thy soul is nourished and at rest: then

138

faith will be as natural as scent to a flower, or bloom to a peach. Do not ask if thy faith is of the right sort; all faith is right, which is directed towards Him, whom God hath set forth to receive the loving devotion of all human hearts.

21

HIS SOUL AN OFFERING FOR SIN

"To the cross He nails thine enemies—
The law that is against thee, and the sins
Of all mankind, with Him there crucified—
Never to hurt them more, who rightly trust
In this His satisfaction."

Milton

(Isaiah 53:10)

It is strange, but it is true, that the saddest, darkest day that ever broke upon our world is destined to cure the sadness, and dissipate the darkness for evermore. It is to the passion of the Redeemer that loving hearts turn in their saddest, darkest, most sin-conscious hours to find solace, light, and help. It is for this reason, doubtless, that Scripture lays such stress on the wondrous cross; and that prophets and evangelists proceed with such deliberation to tell the story of that death, which is the death of death for all who understand its inner meaning.

With what elaborate care the meaning of the cross is wrought out in the chapter under our consideration! As though to obviate the possibility of mistaking its meaning, we are reminded again, and yet again, that the death of the Divine Servant was no ordinary episode; but distinguished from all other deaths, from all martyrdoms and sacrifices, in its unique and lonely grandeur—the one perfect and sufficient sacrifice and oblation for the sins of the whole world. Every form of expression is used to accentuate the thought, that its excessive agony was not the symptom of special sin on the part of the

Sufferer, as the superficial spectator might be disposed to think ; but that He was wounded for our transgressions, bruised for our iniquities, stricken with our stripes, and involved in the penalty which we deserved.

The prophet's thought will become apparent, if we notice, first, the common lot of man ; then the one point in which the experience of Jesus was unique ; and, lastly, apply the sentiment of the text to our own experience.

(1) THE COMMON LOT OF MAN.—It may be summed up in three words—suffering, sin, death. (1) *Suffering.* Nature is fair, but her gladdest scenes cover the suffering that pervades ocean and land. In the woodland glade, where spring has scattered her first wild flowers, you may detect the scream of the rabbit captured by the stoat. From the blue summer sky the eagle swoops down on the pasture lands. The placid surface of the mere is ruffled by the struggles of the minnow to escape the pike. Nature groans and travails in pain ; much more human life.

The boys and girls with their merry laugh and frolic to-day, will to-morrow be bending over the cradle where the wee babe is dying ; or presently bearing the stern discipline which seems an inevitable part of human destiny. You cannot traverse a street without hearing an infant's wail, or visit a home on which there is no shadow. Sooner or later each man has to say, Either I must master or be mastered, either I must vanquish or succumb, in this bitter conflict with the mysterious, all-pervasive, impalpable, yet deadly antagonist, suffering—pain—sorrow unto death. "Man is born to sorrow, as the sparks fly upward." That was the reflection of the wise pensive East, centuries before the wear and tear of modern life began.

(2) *Sin.* We all know this also—the sense of sin, of discord, of distance and alienation from God. Behind all our suffering we feel there is a secret, which somehow explains and accounts for it. We have scorned and perverted that which was right. We have done things we ought not, or left undone things we ought to have done. Men try to evade this consciousness of sin. They plunge into affairs, travel from land to land, go far afield in search of adventure and ceaseless change, give themselves

140

up to gaiety and dissipation. In fact, they are ever eluding the fixed sad gaze of conscience, and adopting any subterfuge which promises a moment's cover. But it comes back again and again. The prophet-voice arraigns us; the inerrant sleuth-hound runs us down. "Thou art the man!"

This sense of sin has covered the world with altars, temples, and churches. Wherever men are found, some religious rite betrays the heavy sense of sin, which is prepared to give rivers of oil or flocks of sheep, yea the very fruit of the body, to stay the gnawings of the heart.

(3) *Death.* The conscience of man connects sin and death by an inevitable sequence. Prior to the writing of the Epistle to the Romans, the older scripture of human experience and observation asserted that death had passed upon all men, for that all had sinned. For this cause, we can never get reconciled to death. Call it by euphemistic titles; talk of it lightly as a transition, a passage, an exodus; speak of the victory which Jesus Christ achieved when He abolished death, and brought life and immortality to light—still we can never dissociate from death the idea of the sin, except for which it need not have been: "In the day that thou eatest thereof, thou shalt surely die."

These three are inevitable factors in human life.

(2) THE NOTABLE EXCEPTION OF THIS CHAPTER.—The Divine Servant presents a noble exception to the lot of man; not in his sufferings, for He was "a Man of Sorrows, and acquainted with grief"; nor in his death, for He died many deaths in one (9, R.V., marg.); but in his perfect innocence and goodness. "He had done no violence, neither was any deceit in his mouth." Let us consider this, and the conclusion to be derived from it. There is sorrow in this chapter, as in all the world. The marred face tells a true tale; for the turbid streams of unknown sorrows have poured into the Sufferer's heart, until it has brimmed to high-water mark. Despised and rejected, wounded and bruised, led to the slaughter and cut off from the land of the living, amid degradation and cruelty, the Divine Servant has passed through every painful experience; has drunk to its dregs every cup; has studied deeply every black-lettered volume in the library of pain.

In his case, at least, man's hastily-formed conclusions are falsified. Generally we pass from singular suffering to discover its cause in some hidden or remote transgression. "Who did sin, this man or his parents, that he was born blind?" Untold anguish has been inflicted through the indiscriminate application of this method. Myriads, like Job, have winced, as the probing knife, wielded by unsympathising hands, has searched the most secret passages of life to discover where the wrong lay that was being avenged. And the sufferer has been made to fear lest he had been unwittingly guilty of an offence against the Infinite God, which could only be expiated by the infliction of excessive chastisement.

In the case of Jesus Christ, however, this explanation of his unique sufferings was altogether at fault. His life was searched with microscopic care, to discover a single flaw to justify his condemnation. The most secret passages of his intercourse with his disciples and friends were ransacked by the keen eye of the traitor, with the object of discovering an excuse for his dark deed. But all was in vain. Pilate and Herod asserted his absolute faultlessness. Finally, He, who of all men was most humble and meek, bared his life to the world with the challenge He knew could never be taken up, "Which of you convinceth Me of sin?" Another explanation must therefore be forthcoming to account for the sufferings of the innocent and spotless Saviour.

This explanation lay hid, as a secret concealed in a hieroglyph, in the vast system of Levitical sacrifice, which foreshadowed the "offering of the body of Jesus Christ once for all." Year by year, myriads of innocent and spotless victims surrendered their lives prematurely, their life-blood flowing freely for no fault of theirs, but on account of the sins of those who brought them to the altar of God. To the most casual observer, and altogether apart from the disclosures of the Epistle to the Hebrews, it was clear that their sufferings were altogether due to sins not their own. This was a light on the one act of Calvary (Rom. 5:8).

Does not the father suffer for his son, as he strips himself to penury to pay his profligate debts? Does not the physician suffer for the sins of others, when he is stricken down in his effort to rescue another from the incidence of disease caused by violating the elementary laws

142

of health? Have not thousands perished in rescuing others from fire and flood? Such actions as these illustrate, though very imperfectly, that of the sinless Saviour pouring out his soul unto death.

So, under the divine guidance, men were led from the conclusions of verse 4 to those of verse 5. Instead of accounting Christ as stricken, smitten of God, and afflicted, they came to see that He had borne their griefs, carried their sorrows, and died for their sins; that He was the Lamb of God, taking away the sins of the world: that his death was the voluntary substitution of Himself for a world of transgressors. These conclusions, expressed here as the verdict of the human conscience, after scanning the facts in the light of history, are confirmed and clenched by the unanimous voice of the New Testament: "He was made sin for us, though He knew no sin." "Through His one act of righteousness, the free gift came unto all men to justification of life."

This is the great exception which has cast a new light on the mystery of pain and sorrow. It may be that there is other suffering, which, in a lower sense and in a smaller measure, is also redemptive, fulfilling Divine purposes in the lives of others; though no sufferer is free from sin as Christ was, and none has ever been able to expiate sin as He. None can ransom his brother's soul.

(3) THE PERSONAL APPLICATION OF THESE TRUTHS.—
"Thou must make his soul a guilt-offering" (R.V., marg.). This term, "guilt-offering," occurs in the Book of Leviticus. If a man committed a trespass in the holy things of the Lord, he was directed to select and bring from his flock a ram without blemish. This was his *guilt-offering* —the word used here. He was to make a money restitution for his offence; but the atonement was made through the ram. "The priest shall make atonement for him with the ram of the guilt-offering, and he shall be forgiven" (Lev. 5:1–16).

Similarly, if a man sinned against his neighbour, either in oppressing him or withholding his dues, or neglecting to restore property which had been entrusted to him, he was not only to make restitution, but to bring his guilt-offering to the Lord—a ram without blemish out of the flock—and the priest made an atonement before the Lord, and he was forgiven concerning whatsoever he had done to be made guilty thereby (Lev. 6:1-7).

Is there one of us who has not committed a trespass and sinned in the holy things of the Lord? Failures in fulfilling his sacred commissions; in yielding time and thought to the cultivation of his holy friendship; in maintaining inviolate the temple of the soul—these come to mind and stop our mouths, so that we stand guilty before God.

Is there one who has not failed in his obligations to neighbour and friend? Even if we have not failed in those specific instances named in the old law; even if our conscience does not accuse us of oppression, or withholding dues, or neglecting to restore—still there may have been serious defalcations from the standard of perfect love. It is so easy to say some contemptuous word which robs another of his meed of honour; or to be silent when we ought to speak in defence and vindication of those who are wrongfully accused. Moses taught that this was sin not against man only, but against God. Restitution was to be made to the one; but an atonement had also to be made to Jehovah. Did not this lead David to cry, when his sin had robbed Uriah's home of its choice jewel, "Against Thee, Thee only, have I sinned, and done this evil in Thy sight"?

How certainly we need to present the guilt-offering! If in his dimmer light the Jew felt his need, how much more we, who know that every sin is not only a mistake but a crime, violating the eternal law of righteousness, and bringing an inevitable penalty, unless it be intercepted and averted by the interposition of another. Explain it how we may, it is a fundamental fact in our inner consciousness, that the sense of sin points to the bar of eternal justice, summons us there, and threatens that we shall not go till we have paid the uttermost farthing. Then we look around for a daysman, a mediator, for one who will not only plead our cause before that high tribunal, but who will interpose to avert the deserved penalty by receiving it into his own bosom.

When the weight of remembered sin presses thee to the earth; when awful sorrow calls to remembrance the almost-forgotten sins of early years; when the searchlight of God's truth shines clear into the dark cave of the soul, revealing the evils that lurk there, as slimy things under the covert of thick darkness; when some terrible fall has mastered thee; when perpetual failure makes thee think that forgiveness is impossible—fear not to seek it from the One whom God hath "exalted with his right hand, to be a Prince and a Saviour ... to give forgiveness of sins" (Acts 5:31).

There is no mention made of the necessity of summoning priestly aid. This is the more remarkable, when we consider the strict Levitical system in which Israel was cradled. It would seem that in the great crisis of its need, the soul of man reverts to an earlier cult, and goes back beyond the elaborate system of the temple to the practice of the patriarchal tent, where each man acted as his own priest, and offered the guilt-offering with his own hand. No third person is needed in thy transactions with God. Jesus is Priest as well as Sacrifice. There is no restriction to thine approach; no barrier against thine intrusion; no veil to be passed by the initiated few. The way into the holiest is made manifest, and with boldness thou mayest "enter in by the blood of Jesus" (Heb. 10:19).

To do so is to secure peace. The proof of the truth of the Gospel is to be found in the absolute rest which overspreads the soul which avails itself of its provisions, and adjusts itself on its strong and steadfast principles. Let a man believe in Jesus Christ—not *about* Him, but *in* Him; not in his death, but in Him who died and rose again—and he will be instantly conscious of a peace that passeth understanding, arising from the depths of his nature, and overspreading it like an evening calm. The peace of the world is from without and superficial; the peace of God is from within and is all-pervading.

In that peace much else is included. Sorrow is not banished from the life, but it becomes radiant with light; suffering is borne with a new resignation and fortitude; pain is welcomed with the blessed conviction that it may have a redemptive quality which shall operate somehow, somewhere; and death is contemplated without alarm. Thus from the darkest day that ever dawned upon our world, have come rays of hope and joy which are ushering in the world in which there is no night, neither sorrow, nor crying, nor pain, nor death; and where God shall wipe the tears from all faces.

And that darkest day in the experience of our blessed

Lord has won for Him a revenue of gladness, which can never be exhausted as the blessed harvest of his tears and blood is reaped by individuals and worlds, He sees his spiritual seed, He finds a multiplication of his life, He realises that the scheme of redemption, which is also the pleasure of his Father, is prospering in his hands.

22

THE SATISFACTION OF THE MESSIAH

> *"He shall reign from pole to pole*
> *With illimitable sway;*
> *He shall reign, when like a scroll*
> *Yonder heavens have passed away.*
> *Then the end; beneath His rod*
> *Man's last enemy shall fall.*
> *Hallelujah! Christ in God,*
> *God in Christ, is all in all."*

Montgomery

(Isaiah 53:11)

Satisfied! Very few can say that word on this side of heaven. The alpine climber cannot, so long as inaccessible summits rear themselves beyond his reach. The conqueror who has overrun the world cannot; he weeps because there are no more worlds to conquer. The philosopher cannot, though he has discovered the hidden harmonies of Nature, and unveiled her ancient order; for his circle of light only extends the circumference of the dark unknown. Even the Christian cannot say it, since he has not yet attained, neither is already perfect. But Christ shall be satisfied, and is already drinking deep draughts of the joy set before Him when He endured the cross, despising its shame.

There is no satisfaction for those who are self-centred; and we say reverently that God Himself could not have known perfect blessedness unless He had been able to

146

pour Himself forth in blessing upon others. We are therefore conscious of a fitness in meeting this allusion to the satisfaction of Christ amidst these words that speak of his sacrifice unto death. Whatever may be the character of that joy which He had with the Father, before the worlds were made, it surely will pale in intrinsic value before that joy which for evermore will accrue to Him as the interest upon his expenditure at Calvary.

We might put the truth into four sentences. There is no satisfaction apart from love. There cannot be love for sinning suffering souls without travail. There cannot be travail without compensating joy. In proportion to the travail, with its pangs and bitterness, will be the resulting blessedness.

(1) THE TRAVAIL OF CHRIST'S SOUL.—He suffered because of his quick sympathy with the anguish that sin had brought to man. He probably saw, as we cannot, the timid oppressed by the strong; the helpless victim pursued by rapacity and passion; mothers weeping over the children that had been torn from their forlorn and desolate hearts. He heard the wail of the world's sorrow, in which cries of little children, the shriek or moan of womanhood, and the deep bass of strong men wrestling with the encircling serpent-folds, mingle in one terrible medley. He sighed over the deaf and dumb, had compassion on the leper, wept at the grave. As the thornbrake to bare feet, so must this world have been to his compassionate heart.

He must also have suffered keenly by the rejection of those whom He would have gathered, as a hen gathers her chickens under her wing, but they would not. Was there a contemptuous name they did not hurl at Him; an insult that did not alight upon his head; an avenue along which man's hate can reach the heart of his fellow-man, which was not trodden bare by those who repaid his love by a hate which had the venom of hell in it, as his love the fragrance of Paradise?

But these elements of pain are not to be compared with that more awful sorrow which He experienced as the substitute and sacrifice of human guilt. In a following verse we are told that "He poured out his soul unto death." It was a voluntary act to which He was nerved by the infinite love that dared to make his soul an offer-

147

ing for sin. What did Jesus suffer on the cross? The physical pain that wracked his body was probably hardly perceptible to Him amid the pressure of those stripes with which we are healed. He was wounded, not in his tender flesh only, but in his holy loving heart. He was bruised between the millstones of God's justice and unswerving fidelity to truth. He was stricken because He received into his soul the penalty of human guilt. He stood before the universe charged with the sins of the race, and their consequence. He tasted death for every man. He was so identified with sin, its shame, suffering, and penalty, that He deemed Himself forsaken by God. In that one act of the cross He put away sin, exhausted the penalty, wiped out the guilt, and laid the foundation of a redemption which includes the whole family of man.

It could not be otherwise. He could not have loved us perfectly without becoming one with us in the dark heritage of our first parent. Son of Man as He was, though Himself sinless, He could not but be involved in the entail of condemnation which was the lot of the human family. With us, and for us, He must suffer. With us, and for us, He must die. With us, and for us, He must meet the demands of a broken law, and satisfy them eternally.

Dost thou love Christ? The first duty He will lay on thee will be love to others. He will tell thee there is no true love for Himself which does not go out for those whom He has loved. The same sentiment of the human heart, which has an aspect towards Him, has at the same time as aspect towards all. And if thou dost truly love, thou too shalt find thy need of soul-travail. Thou too wilt have to go without the camp, bearing his reproach. Thou canst not love men into life without suffering with them, and for them—not to the same extent that Christ suffered, but in thy measure. Think it not strange when that fiery trial comes; but rejoice that thou art called to be a partaker of the sufferings of Christ, that at the revelation of his glory thou mayest rejoice with exceeding joy.

(2) THE CERTAINTY OF INFINITE COMPENSATION.—"He *shall* see." It is impossible to suffer voluntarily for others, and not in some way benefit them. Of course, there is pain in the world which is punitive, deadly. The pain

148

which is the result of pride, that frets and chafes against the rule of the Almighty; like the sea churning itself in yeasty rage at the foot of the cliffs. The pain of those that fling themselves on the serried ranks of God's order and law; like the French cuirassiers on the English squares on the field of Waterloo. The pain of those that suffer for the pain they have themselves inflicted.

There is other pain which is remedial and life-giving. The pain of the mother bringing forth her first-born. The pain of the woman's nature that clings to a prodigal —husband, brother, or son—sharing his shame; agonising in his repeated outbreaks; and by tears, prayers, and sacrifice, winning him for God. The pain of nature, groaning and travailing with the genesis of the new heavens and earth. The pain of the Saviour, giving life and salvation to myriads born again into the Kingdom. The pain of the Spirit, groaning within the saints, and ushering in the Church of the First-born. The pain of the children of God, who groan within themselves, waiting for the adoption, to wit, the redemption of the body.

The earth is full of each kind of pain; but the first is characteristic of the first Adam; the last, of the Second. The first belongs to an order which is destined to vanish away; the last to an age, the dawn of which, as sighted from the highest peaks of saintliness, is fairer than any light which has ever broken on the eyes or hearts of man. Woe be to thee, O son of man, if thou knowest nothing of this blessed travail; if thou hast never known what it is to be in anguish for the souls of others; if thy bosom has never been rent with strong cryings and tears; if thou hast never known the wish to be accurst from God, so that thou mightest win thy brethren according to the flesh! Blessed art thou if thou knowest aught hereof! Thy pain may sometimes seem abortive —the mighty throes that rend thee for the souls of others appear in vain; but it is not really so. Drop by drop thy tears shall presently turn the scale. Patience shall have her perfect work. The laws of the harvest in this sphere are as certain in their operation as in that of nature. God guarantees the results. He is faithful. Thou shalt come again, bringing thy sheaves with thee: they that sow in tears shall reap in joy. In the golden future, if not before, thou shalt meet again each tear and sigh, and pang and prayer, transfigured in the result.

149

(3) THE NATURE OF CHRIST'S COMPENSATION.—It will come: (1) *In the glory that shall accrue to the Father.* It has been the one aim of the Second Person in the Holy Trinity, to reveal the character and glory of the First, that all intelligent and holy beings may love Him. He has done this in creation; in the government of the worlds; but, above all, in his cross. There we behold righteousness and peace kissing each other; the wisdom that invented a way of salvation consistent with the claim of moral law; the faithfulness which, in the fulness of the times, fulfilled the earliest promise; and, above all, God's love. To Calvary shall wend the intelligences of every sphere, to acquire new and enlarged conceptions of the Divine character. And as age after age increased powers of vision reveal fresh wonders in the Cross, Christ shall see of the travail of his soul.

(2) *In the redemption of untold myriads.* Great as the harvest of sin has been, we believe that the saved shall vastly outnumber the lost. Nothing less will satisfy Christ. Remember that in the first age, before mention is made of the latter triumphs of the Gospel, John beheld in heaven a multitude which no man could number. This was but the first-fruit sheaf; let who will compute the full measure of the harvest! The martyr throng; the Christians who were recognised by no fellow-believer, and numbered in no church; the babes caught to his bosom; the Godly souls in every nation, like Cornelius, who have been saved by virtue of a death of which they never heard; the myriads that shall be gathered in during the Millennial age—*these* are streamlets that shall swell the river of the ransomed to overflowing. In them shall Christ see of the travail of his soul, and be satisfied.

(3) *In the character of the redeemed.* He shall present them to Himself without spot, or wrinkle, or any such thing. He shall present them to his Father with exceeding joy; the devil's handmark obliterated from their character; the Father's image complete. Think you when Jesus takes to Himself his peerless Bride, purchased by his blood, sanctified by his spirit, adorned in her marriage array—that He will not see of the travail of his soul, and be satisfied?

(4) *In the destruction of the devil's work.* What is involved in the majestic promise that He should destroy

the works of the devil, is not yet made manifest. In due time we shall see it all. The mists that now veil the landscape, the scaffolding which hides the building, will be removed. We shall see what God means. The curse gone from nature. Grace abounding much more where sin and death had reigned. Man lifted nearer God than he could have been had he dwelt for ever in an unsullied paradise. The kingdoms of the world, and of all other worlds, become the kingdoms of our God and of his Christ. Then, as the hallelujah chorus breaks from millions—like the triumphant shout from the lips of the emancipated Israel ; as the waves of harmony break around the sapphire throne in tumultuous melody ; as the forms of monster evils lie strewn around the shores of the crystal sea mingled with fire—Christ shall see of the travail of his soul, and be satisfied.

(4) THE GREATNESS OF THOSE RESULTS.—(1) *They must be proportionate to the glory of his nature*. It is not difficult to satisfy, at least temporarily, a little child. Imperfect knowledge will hush its curiosity, trifling toys please its fancy. But as its nature develops, it becomes increasingly hard to content it.

But surely there is more difference between the capacity of an angel and that of a man, than between the capacities of a man and a babe. If a man requires for his satisfaction more than a child, how much must not the capacious bosom of an angel need! The power for which men contend is child's play, to those who control the rush of winds, and regulate the motion of worlds! The knowledge that men esteem as marvellous, to an angel is but the prattling of a babe. How much would have to be accumulated, ere an angel could say, "It is enough, I am satisfied"! But, great as an angel is, his capacity is limited and finite. What then must be the measure of that blessedness, of that harvest of souls, of that result of his travail, which can content the Divine Redeemer? His nature is so vast that nothing short of a seed like the stars in the sky, or the sand on the shore can satisfy.

The immeasureableness of the results of redemption can only be estimated by those who consider the immeasureableness of the Divine nature of the Redeemer.

(2) *They must be proportionate to the intensity of his suffering*. The results of God's work are always com-

151

mensurate to the force He puts forth. You cannot imagine the Divine Being going to an immense expenditure without a sure prescience that He would be recouped. When He puts his hands to a work, it is because He knows that He can carry it through, and that the golden gain will be satisfactory remuneration. When therefore we behold the Son of Man emptying Himself, stooping to the humiliation of Bethlehem, the anguish of Golgotha, the death of Calvary, we know that the spoils which will fall to his share, when He divides them with the strong, will not be unworthy or inadequate.

Satisfied! We shall hear his sigh of deep content, and see the triumph on his face. We shall witness the sublime transference of the kingdom to God, even the Father. We shall see the satisfactory termination of the mystery of evil. And if Christ is satisfied, we shall be. On this let us rest. And when our hearts misgive us because of the waste and havoc, the tears of blood, the awful suffering, that sin has brought into the universe of God, let us assure ourselves that all will yet be well ; and that we shall drink deep draughts of the satisfaction of our Lord, when we see of the travail of his soul, and are satisfied.

23

THE GREATNESS OF THE SIN-BEARER

"We must not stand to gaze too long,
Though on unfolding Heaven our gaze we bend,
Where lost behind the bright angelic throng
We see Christ's entering triumph slow ascend.

"No fear but we shall soon behold,
Faster than now it fades, that gleam revive,
When issuing from his cloud of fiery gold
Our wasted frames feel the true Sun, and live."

Keble

(Isaiah 53 : 12)

It is impossible to mistake the majestic personality speaking through the pronoun "I." It is the voice of God Himself ; and it is befitting that, as He introduced his Servant in the opening verses of this marvellous portraiture, so, in these closing words, He should pronounce his verdict on His career. We have watched, as the chapter has unfolded, how the opinion of the speaker and others, being represented by this *we*, passed through many phases—hostility, criticism, pity—before it settled to penitence and faith. In this respect it is a true delineation of the attitiude of the world generally towards Jesus of Nazareth, who realised this unique ideal; and, surely, the words on which we are now to dwell anticipate the verdict of the Eternal, when the mystery of sin and suffering is over for ever, and time is running out to its last day.

Two things are clearly predicated of the Sin-Bearer. First, that He should be great; and secondly, that He should attain his commanding position, not as the founder of a new school of thought, nor as the leader of a social reformation, nor as possessed of exceptional saintliness —but as a Sufferer.

This should be clearly noted. It is because "He poured out his soul unto death"—a phrase which calls attention to the voluntary and moral aspects of his sufferings; because He allowed Himself to be numbered amongst the transgressors, not as naturally, but as sympathetically, one with them ; because He interceded for them, as standing beside them and identified in their interests—that the Almighty Father gives Him a portion with the great, and causes Him to divide the spoil with the strong.

We are not dealing here with the glory He had with the Father before the worlds were made. Of this He emptied Himself when He became obedient unto the death of the cross ; and though now He has resumed it, yet the greatness which He obtained through death is not only his greatest boast, but must always have the greatest intrinsic interest for us.

(1) THE GREATNESS GIVEN BY THE FATHER AS THE REWARD FOR CHRIST'S OBEDIENCE TO DEATH.—It was meet that such a reward should be bestowed, for the sake of those who should afterwards follow in the footsteps of their Divine Master. Here was One who never swerved from the narrow track of obedience, whose course glorified and magnified the character of God ; if it could be shown that such unparalleled devotion was fruitless and unrecognised, that it was treated with complete indiffer-

ence, whilst the faithful Servant was permitted to lie in an unknown and dishonoured grave, would it not daunt other ardent souls, bent on following his example, forcing them to feel that the interests of God were antagonistic to those of Man? None could ever deserve more or better than Christ; and if He were without recognition or reward, might it not be thought that heaven had no prize to give for faithful service? Surely He must have a reward, or the very order of the universe might be deemed at fault!

But what reward should He have? What could compensate Him for having laid aside the exercise of his Divine prerogative; for having assumed our nature; for having passed through the ordeal of temptation, sorrow, and pain; for having become obedient to death, even the death of the cross? All worlds were his by native right; all holy beings owned his sway as Creator and God; all provinces of thought, emotion, power, and might, sent Him their choicest tribute. What reward could He claim, or have?

The answer may be suggested by recalling our own pleasure in conferring pleasure, our joy in giving joy. To bless, to save, to help another, will fill our bosom with the most unalloyed blessedness of which the heart of man is capable. But our power, as well as our capacity, is limited; we cannot do as we would. Let, however, the limitations imposed by our mortality or circumstances be removed; let us be able to realise to the full the yearnings and promptings of our noblest hours; let the wish to help be accompanied by a sympathy that cannot hurt the most sensitive, a wisdom that cannot mistake, a power that cannot be daunted or thwarted; and probably we should at once drink deep draughts of blessedness like God's.

This is the blessedness of Christ, and this the reward which the Father has given Him. All power is given Him, in heaven and on earth, because He is the Son of Man, and can use it for the unmixed benefit of those whom He has, in such wonderful condescension, made his brothers. He is raised to the right hand of the Father, that He may requite with coals of fire the nation that rejected and crucified Him, by giving repentance and remission of sins. God has given Him a name—the name Jesus, Saviour—which is above every name, that in it and through it every knee should bow, and every tongue confess that He is Lord, to the glory of the Father. All that come to Him may now be saved, even to the uttermost. All that yield to Him are delivered from the power of darkness, and translated into the Kingdom of God's love. To the furthest limit of its meaning, He is able to realise his own prayer, that the essential oneness and blessedness of the Divine nature should be realised in those who believe.

God Himself could not give, nor the Saviour ask for, a greater reward than this. And, in its magnificence, it appeals to all who would tread in his steps. The closer we approach Him in his self-sacrifice, the more fully we shall attain to his recompense. The deeper we drink of his cup, and are baptized with his baptism, the more we shall be able, in our measure, to assist Him in his redemptive purpose. This is what He meant when He spoke of sitting with Him on his throne, and ruling the cities of men in the interests of purity, righteousness, and peace.

Ask Paul why he was so eager to keep under his body, in his zeal making it black and blue with blows; why he denied himself legitimate gratification; why he was so abstemious and self-denying: and he will confess that it arises from his supreme desire, lest, having proclaimed as a herald the rules of the contest for others, he may miss the prize. And if you inquire further of what that prize consisted, he will modestly tell you that its charm and value to him lie in the greater power that it will confer of saving others (1 Cor. 9:20–27).

This is Heaven's supreme reward: that all who pour out their souls to death shall obtain enlarged opportunities and possibilities of service. It is clear that they will not abuse them to their own hurt. It is equally certain that the exercise of such prerogatives will ensure the richest and most unalloyed blessedness for those by whom they are exerted.

(2) THE GREATNESS THAT CHRIST'S DEATH HAS SECURED HIM AMONG MEN.—He is worthy to take the mysterious scroll of destiny, and break its seals, because of the light He has cast on the great mysteries by which our lot is shadowed.

(1) *Pain.* As we have sadly learnt, it is ubiquitous. Sooner or later it finds us out. And when it enwraps us in its fiery baptism, we are apt to accuse ourselves or to

155

doubt God. "Hast thou come, O sting of fire, to bring my sin to remembrance, and avenge the sins of my youth?" Such is our cry under the first of these impressions. "God is unjust or careless, or He would never let one of his innocent children suffer thus. There is no righteousness in his government of the world. I will curse Him and die." Such is our cry under the second.

But Jesus has taught us that there is yet a third way of regarding pain. He had not sinned, yet He suffered as none of woman-born ever did. Evidently, then, pain is not always symptomatic of special sin. He was once so submerged in anguish that for a time He lost the sense of his Father's love: but He never suggested that there was failure or obliquity in the moral government of the world. The death of Jesus has therefore robbed death of these two implications, and has taught us that it is often sent, and must be borne, with the view of benefiting others. Just because God loves our race, and desires to save and enrich it, He calls some, yea, many, apart from its ranks, and causes them to drink the cup of pain, so that inestimable benefits may accrue to all.

Whenever, therefore, we are called to suffer, especially if unconscious of special sinnership, let us not charge God foolishly; but consider that somehow and somewhere our patient and heroic endurance of anguish, whether physical or mental, will certainly conduce to the furtherance of those redemptive purposes which fill the heart of Jesus—purposes in the sacred partnership of which He has called us to take a share.

What a priceless service was this—to transform pain; to persuade sufferers that by their travail of soul they were enriching the whole world of men; to show the persecuted, the victims of human passion and lust, the paralysed, cancer-eaten, and bedridden, that they had an opportunity of co-operating with the Prince of Sufferers in the overthrow of the dark tyranny which has been fraught with such unutterable agony for them and for myriads! For this we count Christ great, that through his death He has transfigured pain.

(2) *Death*. Men dread it. It is the inevitable shadow which creeps over the warmest sunshine, and silences the gladdest joy. But He, by his dying, has abolished death, and brought life and immortality to light. He

156

spoke of going to his Father; of reunion with his own, on the other side of death, in paradise; of coming again to receive his own to Himself. He showed that there was a track threading the drear valley, which He could pass and repass until all his sheep were safely folded. He had no fear Himself, and taught us to have none. It was the way home, that was all.

Before Jesus came, men had hoped and dreamt that this was so. Still no one knew. Their prognostications were like those of Columbus before he turned his prow westwards, and ploughed the first furrow across the Atlantic. But when Jesus rose, death and resurrection were no longer matters for reasoning or speculation; that fact spoke to all ages as the guesses of philosophers never could have done. Life and immortality were brought to light. For this, therefore, we count Him great, that through death He undid death.

(3) *Sin*. When Jesus died on the cross, He was numbered with transgressors; but He stood over against all transgressors, distinct from them and bearing their sin. The sin of the race was imputed to Him. The guilt and penalty accruing to us all, in consequence of our connection with Adam's fallen family, were borne by Him. As God's Lamb He bore the sin of the world. As man's scapegoat He bore it into a land of forgetfulness, whence it could never again be recovered.

Nay, more, He bore *our* sins in his own body on the tree. Not *sin* alone, as the common heritage of the race; but *sins* also—thine and mine: so that if we confess them with humility and penitence, we may receive immediate and abundant pardon—a pardon which does not violate, but is guaranteed by the faithfulness and justice of God. He must be faithful to his promises, and just to his Son. The natural and secondary consequences remain, although transfigured; but the penal ones are for ever gone, having been exhausted when He gave Himself a ransom and sacrifice for us all. This surely constitutes an overmastering claim for us to count Christ great. In his death He finished transgression; made an end of sins; purged away iniquity; and brought in everlasting righteousness. Thou art worthy, O Lamb of God; for Thou wast slain, and hast redeemed us to God by Thy blood.

(3) THE GREATNESS WHICH HIS DEATH WILL WIN FOR CHRIST IN THE ESTIMATION OF OTHER RACES OF BEING.—Not to the Mount of Beatitudes, but to the Cross, will distant worlds send their deputations in all coming ages, to learn the manifold lessons which it alone can teach. There they will learn to know the very heart of God, his hatred against sin, his love for the sinner, his fidelity to covenant engagements, his righteousness, his truth. The Cross is the heavenly prism that enables us to distinguish the constituents of the Divine nature. There they will be amazed to discover the devotion of Divine love, which could stoop to such humiliation and suffering to win its Bride. There they will gladly recognise the victory of the Son of God over all the malice and power of the enemy.

The volcano of hell has, perhaps for ages, belched out its fury on the universe, to its great detriment and misery ; but since Jesus died and rose, it has been made manifest that its power is broken—its empire at an end. What a relief to the whole moral universe! For what Jesus did on his cross pertains not to men only, but to all races and orders of beings, to whom it proclaims peace. Having made peace through the blood of his cross He shall finally reconcile all things to Himself ; whether things upon the earth, or things in the heavens.

24

"SING, O BARREN!"

"Howbeit, all is not lost.
The warm noon ends in frost ...
Yet through the silence shall
Pierce the Death-Angel's call,
And 'Come up hither,' recover all.
Heart, wilt thou go?—'I go:
Broken hearts triumph so!' "

E. B. Browning

(Isaiah 54:1)

In the previous chapters we have heard the exiles summoned to leave Babylon, and beheld the Divine Servant becoming the Sin-Bearer for them and for the world. Here our attention is startlingly recalled to the desolate city of Jerusalem. "Barren"; "Forsaken"; "Desolate"—such are the terms applied to her by One who cannot err. And they are corroborated by the testimony of a contemporary. "Then said I unto them," is the faithful record of Nehemiah, "Ye see the evil case that we are in, how Jerusalem lieth waste, and the gates thereof are burned with fire" (Neh. 1:3; 2:3, 13–17).

But how is this? Have we not learnt that the Mediator has put away sin at the cost to Himself of wounds and bruises, stripes and death? How then does this city lie as an open sore on the face of the earth? Cannot God's forgiveness, that has triumphed over sin, also triumph over the wreck and ruin that sin has caused? Is that redemption complete which fails to grapple with all the results and consequences of wrong-doing?

This opens up a great subject, and one that touches us all. We are conscious that though our sin is forgiven, yet certain consequences remain, of which that ruined city is a type. We cannot undo the past; God Himself cannot undo it. It can never be as though it had never been. The seventy years of captivity, the shame, the sorrow, the anguish to God, the forfeited opportunities, the thistledown so thoughtlessly scattered! Ah me! God can forgive; but these things cannot be altered now. But what is meant by that word *Redeemer*? What is the meaning of the passage which asserts that where sin reigned unto death, *there* grace would reign unto eternal life? What is meant by the promise of fir-trees instead of thorns, of myrtles instead of briars? These questions are often asked in spirit, if not in so many words; and it is well to attempt an answer. They open up the great subject of the natural consequences of sin, and how God deals with them.

(1) THE NATURAL CONSEQUENCES OF SIN.—(1) *We must distinguish between them and the punitive or penal.* Suppose that a man is taken into custody for being drunk and disorderly. There are two results of that outbreak of uncontrolled passion; on the one hand he has broken the law of his country, for which a penalty of imprisonment or fine must be inflicted; but on the other, and in addition, he has brought on himself the racking headache, the depression of spirits, the awful nervous reaction, which is the natural and inevitable result. These will pursue and scourge him as with the whip of the furies, even when his standing is adjusted with his country's laws.

So, when we sin against God, two consequences accrue. Our sin cries against us, as Abel's blood against Cain; its voice goes up to high heaven, and can only be stilled and hushed by the pleading of the blood of Jesus. It is only as we take that precious blood in hand, and bear it with us into the holiest, presenting it as our propitiation, that we find peace, and rest, and deliverance, both from the guilt and the penalty that would otherwise accrue to us. But when this has been effected, and we are forgiven, accepted, and blessed, there are yet other results to be faced. The drunkard may be forgiven; but his health is undermined, his fortune impaired: he can never be what he would have been had he lived soberly.

Take the case of a man who, in his devotion to politics or society, has sinned against the laws of the home. Night after night he has been away from his young children, till they regard him as a stranger. There is none of that wholesome companionship, that trust, which are such sacred ties, and make the man the father of the household. The mother cannot supply the firmness and strength which the young life needs. Almost insensibly the family grows away from him; and after a few years, when disappointment drives him back, he finds, to his infinite regret, that the love of the children has gone beyond recall. The boys are now men, and seek their pleasures outside the home; the girls think it irksome to while away his weary hours by their society. Now he sees his mistake, and tries to remedy it; but it is too late. He is forgiven by his God, and his wife, who never ceased to cling to him; but he cannot get back that forfeited love. This is his ruined Jerusalem.

(2) *This distinction is Scriptural.* One illustration will be sufficient. When, in response to Nathan's parable, David broke the long silence, and cried, "I have sinned!" the prophet immediately answered, "The Lord hath put away thy sin"; but he added, "The sword shall never depart out of thy house." So far as the sin lay between God and David's soul, it was removed immediately on his confession; but, so far as the natural consequences were concerned, they followed him for many a long year. The death of Bathsheba's babe, the murder of Amnon, the revolt of Absalom, the rending of the kingdom, were the harvest of which that sin was the autumn sowing.

We need not reiterate the lessons of this chapter; but only recall the assurance of the fortieth chapter, that Jerusalem's iniquity has been pardoned, and contrast it with the allusions of this chapter to its desolate ruins and waste. It is clear then that we may, through penitence and faith, realise the perfect pardon of our Saviour; and yet there may be the hideous waste, the scar, the lost years, of which this ruined city was so significant.

(3) *These natural consequences are bitter to bear.* The enumeration, as given here, reminds us of Marah, before the tree—true emblem of the cross—had, by the Divine direction, been cast into the waters. To bear no children; to work without result; to have little sense of the presence of God; to suffer in mind, or nerve, or circumstance, or, worse than all, in the lives of others—these are among the natural consequences of sin, and are frought with anguish sometimes through long years. Let us remember the inevitableness and bitterness of these results, when tempted to the indulgence of passion. It is quite true that

one look of confession and faith will secure reinstatement in the favour of God; but it is also true that what a man sows he must reap. And though he be a Christian, accepted and forgiven, if he sows of the flesh, he must reap.

(2) HOW GOD OVERRULES SIN'S NATURAL CONSEQUENCES.—Jehovah says, *"Sing."* "Sing, O barren; break forth into singing, and cry aloud!"

"How can I sing?" says Israel; "my city is in ruins; my temple burned with fire; my precious things laid waste. How can I sing?"

"Nevertheless," is the Divine reply, "the time for singing is come. Sing, not because of what thou hast; but of what I have promised to give. Enlarge the place of thy tent; lengthen thy cords; strengthen thy stakes; make room for the incoming of a great host that shall own thee mother."

"But the results of our backslidings remain. Thou canst not undo them, though Thou mayest forgive. Thou canst not give us back the seventy years of exile. Thou canst not obliterate the scar of bruise and wound and sore. Thou canst not intercept the inevitable recoil of our sins."

Yet Jehovah answers, "O barren one! thou must sing as thou didst when thou camest from Egypt. Not with the same exuberant joy; but with a deeper insight into that grace which, in addition to its abundant pardon, can transform the irreparable past, transmuting its briars to myrtles, and its thorns to fig-trees, bringing good out of evil, transforming 'Benonis,' sons of sorrow, into 'Benjamins,' sons of the right hand."

So God our Father is able to make men and women in middle life sing again, as in the days of their youth, with a joy chastened by their memory of the failures and transgressions, which yet have yielded honey like the carcase of Samson's lion. As in the great world, Adam's sin has been overruled to the great enrichment of the race, so in the small world of our individual experience, we rise by our falls; triumph in our defeats; and through the experience of the wilderness enter into the land of rest.

Let us illustrate this in the history of the exile. Terrible as was the immediate loss inflicted by the national back-sliding, demanding the penalty of the captivity, yet in three respects that captivity was overruled to enrich the religious life of the chosen people, and ultimately of the world.

(1) They conceived new and enlarged ideas of God. Before that time, they had thought of Him as a local and national Deity, like the gods of the nations around; now they learnt that the Holy One of Israel should be called the God of the whole earth (verse 5).

(2) They understood better the nature of true religion. Before the captivity, in the estimation of the majority of the Jewish people, it consisted in rites and ceremonies and outward observances ; but when there was no temple, altar, or priest, and still the prophets exhorted them to godliness, it became apparent to the least thoughtful, that true and undefiled religion was independent of the material and sensuous, and demanded only God and the soul. In the captivity we first meet with the institution of the synagogue, where devout souls could worship God in simplicity and spirituality.

(3) They realised their world-wide mission. On the thought of the chosen people rose the dawn of a new conception of the purposes of God in their calling and discipline: they were to be as the dew of the Lord on the earth, disseminating everywhere those blessed truths of which they were the Divinely chosen custodians, and enlarging their tent to include the Gentiles (Gal. 4:27). There was a sense, therefore, in which their casting-away was the reconciling of the world.

Such were the results of their exile, God's grace touched the darkness and blackness of their righteously-deserved afflictions, and transmuted them to gold. So, still ; the forgiven drunkard can never undo the ravage to health or fortune ; but he is made humble, thoughtful, intent on saving those who are under the same spell as he was. The violator of the laws of the homelife becomes more tender, more unselfish, more refined and sensi-tive in the love he gives, than he would have been till disappointment and heart-hunger had done their perfect work. In those who have suffered from the results of their sins, there is a humility, tenderness, softness in speech, delicacy in understanding the temptations and failures of others, the soul of the prophet, the intercession of the priest, which are beyond price. The pardoned prodigal can talk of his Father's love in a way that the elder son

163

could never do ; and as we hear him speak, we know that he is enriching us with spoils gathered by his experiences in the far country.

Whilst we mourn our sins, and bitterly lament their cost and pain, yet we can see how God is at work taking up the very waste of our lives and making it up again into the fairest fabrics; as rich dyes are made from the produce of gas-retorts, and white paper from old and disused rags. In our exile we get new thoughts of God, of religion, and of our mission among men. Probably we should have reached them in some other way had we never wandered ; but we may have learnt them under conditions which will for ever give a special flavour and tone to our affirmation of these mighty truths.

(3) WORDS OF HELP TO ANY WHO MAY BE SUFFERING FROM THE RESULTS OF PAST WRONG-DOING.—The past cannot be altered ; but it is a comfort to know that it can be forgiven, and the soul made white and clean. These great blessings should not be lost sight of amid the outbursts of an infinite regret.

There is a world of difference also between punishment and chastisement. The one is for the Saviour, who bore the guilt and penalty for man on the cross ; the other only is for us who are one with Him by a living faith. Let us not say we are being punished, when the recoil of past transgression strikes us with mailed hand: but that we are being chastened so as to escape condemnation with the world. The same circumstances that are punitive to the ungodly, are disciplinary to the child of God. Our Father chastens us for our profit, using as his rod the natural consequences of our sins.

At such times God calls us back to Himself as a wife forsaken and grieved in spirit. He knows the disappointment and shame of the downcast soul (6). He waits to *gather* with great mercies, and to show mercy with everlasting kindness (7, 8). Let us heed his call, and return to Him ; not allowing the sorrows and sufferings we endure to alienate us, but counting them as opportunities for claiming more of his aid.

We must also believe in his inalienable love. His is our Husband still, and cannot put us away from Him ; the kindness with which He has had mercy on us is everlasting ; He has even sworn that the waters of death and destruction shall not for ever separate us from Him; He has entered into a covenant of peace with us which shall outlast the mountains and the hills. We may grow apathetic and careless, bringing to ourselves pain and woe; grieving and dishonouring Him, and hindering the development of his purposes. But He cannot cease to love. His tender pity will still embrace us; grieving to see our self-inflicted sorrows, but using them as a furnace, the fervent heat of which will consume our bonds, whilst it leaves our skin unscorched, and the hairs of our head unsinged.

If I ascend into heaven, Thy love is there; but if I make my bed in hell, it is there also. If I take the wings of the morning, and dwell in the uttermost part of the sea, placing it as a great gulf of separation between Thee and me, there shall Thy hand lead me, and Thy right hand uphold me. If I say, Surely the darkness shall cover me, even the night shall be light around me; and through it Thou shalt follow every step, leading me back to Thyself, and through my very wanderings accomplishing the loftiest purposes for my purity and holiness. Such love is too wonderful for me, I cannot attain unto it; but I will lie down and rest in its everlasting arms.

25

THE CITY OF GOD

"Far o'er yon horizon
Rise the city towers,
Where our God abideth;
That fair home is ours!
Flash the streets with jasper,
Shine the gates with gold,
Flows the gladdening river,
Shedding joys untold."

Dean Alford

(Isaiah 54: 11)

The reference is still to Jerusalem. In the former paragraph, she was addressed as a barren wife; here is destined to arise from her encumbering ruins, and become the joy of the whole earth. Of course, the primary reference is to that actual rebuilding which took place under the direction of the good Nehemiah. But there is a further and more spiritual meaning. These words must refer to that city of God which is ever arising amid the ruins of all other structures. Watched by the ever-attentive eye of the great Architect, wrought by unseen hands, tested by the constant application of the line of truth and the plummet of righteousness, and emerging slowly from heaps of rubbish into strength and beauty.

A description is given of the pricelessness of the structure, the privileges of the inhabitants, and the safety which is assured by the Word of God; and let us not hesitate to appropriate this blessed vision. It is put clearly within our reach by the assurance with which the chapter closes, that this is the heritage of all the servants of the Lord.

(1) THE PRICELESSNESS OF THE STRUCTURE.—What an enumeration of precious stones! The sapphire, the ruby, the agate, and the carbuncle, vie with each other, and flash with varied but resplendent colour. Now, let us consider what jewels are. They are by nature only lumps of dull and inert matter ; the sapphire is clay, the diamond is carbon. But why the difference between their appearance and that of the ordinary soil? The answer is not easy to give ; but this exquisite effect is probably due to crystallisation, conducted under exceptional circumstances of convulsion, pressure, and fire. A jewel is a bit of ordinary earth which has passed through an extraordinary experience. Thus there is a special fitness in this address to the afflicted people of God—theirs are the convulsions ; theirs the awful pressure ; theirs the fiery baptism. They count it hard—they cannot understand why they are treated thus. But they will see it all one day, when they learn that God was making agates for windows, carbuncles for gates, and sapphires for foundations.

Foundations of sapphires. The sapphire is one of the fairest of jewels. It is born in the darkness ; but it hides the secret of the rarest beauty at its heart. The blue of the sapphire perpetuates in unfading hues the loveliness of the gentian, the violet, and the forget-me-not ; of the summer-sky and the summer-sea ; and of the glacier-depth, where perhaps the deepest blue is to be seen in the walls of ice-rock. It is frequently mentioned in Scripture. The elders saw a pavement of sapphire under the feet of the God of Israel. It was fifth among the precious stones in the breastplate, and second among the foundations of the New Jerusalem. Blue is the most prevalent colour in Nature, forming the background of sea, and sky, and distance; it also predominated in the tabernacle and temple, when it was always coupled with gold in the description of the sacred furniture. As the gold was emblematic of the glory and majesty of God, so was blue of his love and grace in Jesus.

It is very suggestive to be told that the foundations of the Divine structure are laid with sapphires. *They are full of love:* the sapphire is the emblem of love; and underneath our lives, underpinning the history of the world of men, the one ultimate fact for us all is the love of God. Go down as deep and as far as you will, you must come at last to the bed-rock of God's love in Christ. *They are stable:* jewels are the most lasting of all earthly objects, as imperishable as they are beautiful. Such is the basis of Christian hope. Not a dream of the fancy; not a structure of clouds, which a puff of wind may hurl into red ruin; or a pictured reflection of giant mountain forms on the bosom of the lake, which may be destroyed by the fitful breeze: but enduring and eternal as the throne of God. *They are fair:* the loveliness of God's world is not only in what meets the eye, but reaches into the unseen. Not only does He lavish beauty on flowers, and woodlands, and outspread landscapes; but on the massive foundations of the earth, where lie the pure white quartz, the granite and porphyry, with their rich veins and colours. But how fair are the foundations of our religion!—the covenant made in the council chamber of eternity; the blood of the atonement; the identification of the Redeemer with the lost; the eternal purpose which from all ages God has purposed in Himself that grace shall conquer sin.

Windows of agates. Agates are varieties of quartz, and bear evidently in their texture the mark of fire. Indeed, they are always found in the igneous rocks, from which they drop out when such rocks decompose under the action of water and air. The agate is partially transpar-

ent: not opaque, as flint; not transparent, as rock-crystal
—it admits light, tempering it as it passes.

God makes windows of agates; that may be interpreted
to mean that He takes our sorrows and makes them windows through which we may gaze into the unseen. We
shall not in this world see eye to eye, or know as we are
known. The medium of our seeing will always be partially
obscured. But let us be very grateful that we can see at
all. In sorrow we see the unsatisfying nature of the
world, and the reality of the unseen; we learn to appreciate the tenderness and delicacy of human love;
we have insight into the meaning of God's providences;
we behold the value and truth of Scripture. Windows of
agates, but still windows. O tossed with tempest and not
comforted, thou wilt yet have to praise thy God that
thou wert passed through the fire, if only that thou
mightest see!

Gates of carbuncles. There is a good deal of uncer-
tainty as to the precise stone indicated by the Hebrew
word rendered "carbuncle." It seems better, therefore,
to take the suggestion of the duplicate vision in the Apocalypse, and to think of *Gates of pearl.* The pearl is said
to result from the infliction of a wound in the oyster,
which leads it to throw out the precious fluid that con-
geals into a pearl. If so, every pearl on the neck of beauty
is the lasting memento of a stab of pain. At any rate,
each pearl commemorates the hazard of human life in
the diver's descent into the ocean depths. Think of gates
brought from the heart of the sea, each due to the action
of suffering and at the risk of precious life. It is true
of life; all our outgoings into wider ministry, nobler life,
greater responsibility of blessedness, are due to the precious action of sorrow, self-sacrifice, and pain. There is
no gate into the life, which is life indeed, which has not
cost us dear. God makes our pearls into gates, and our
gates of pearls.

When next thou art overwhelmed in sorrow and pain,
or tossed with tempest and not comforted, dare to look
to the outcome of thy stern discipline. It is not for
the present joyous, but grievous; nevertheless *afterward.*
... Our light affliction, which is for the moment, is like
a shaft which it is difficult to turn—it strains thy every
nerve; but on the other side of the wall it is grinding

golden grain, the quality and weight of which will more than compensate thee. Learn then, to look on God as making pleasant stones for the borders of thy life—the walls of salvation and the gates of praise. Is it not a blessed thing to realise that God is making jewels out of very common materials through the fire of trial and pain?

(2) THE PRIVILEGES OF THE CITY: THEY SHALL BE ALL TAUGHT OF GOD.—Our blessed Lord quoted this promise in one of his greatest utterances. "It is written in the prophets," He said, "And they shall be all taught of God. Every man therefore that hath heard, and hath learned of the Father, cometh unto Me" (John 6:45). It is a deep and helpful thought that God has opened a school in this dark world, and has Himself undertaken to act as Schoolmaster. He delegates to no inferior hand the sublime work of educating the human soul. But, fear not! it is the *Father* who teaches. He knows our frame, and remembers that we are dust. Alas, that so many hear and do not learn! There is a great contrast between these two.

How often, when we were at school, in the long summer days—far away now, when days were long—and the door stood open into the garden, our eyes have strayed from book, or copy, or slate, after the butterflies hovering over the flowers, and the big bees droning lazily past; attracted by the rabbits running across the path, and the birds flitting to and fro! We have heard, but not learned; and the lesson has been turned back. Oh, the irksomeness of those turned lessons, when all Nature awaited us outside! So do we evade those Divine lessons, given on the pages of Scripture, of conscience, or of human life, and inculcated by the Divinest tenderness. Did we truly learn of the Father, we should inevitably get to the feet of Jesus. When men say that they believe in God, but not in Jesus Christ whom He has sent, they consciously or unconsciously depart from the truth. The sincere Deist, when Christ is presented, must come to Him.

To be taught of God, to be led by his own hand into a perfect knowledge of the mysteries of Redemption, to sit at the footstep of his throne, to be a pupil in his school, to be his disciple, to have all that the psalmist so repeatedly asked when he cried, "Teach me Thy statutes;

169

lead me in Thy way and teach me"—this is the first of the blessed privileges of the children of the city of God.

Great shall be the peace of thy children. We have first peace with God, through faith in the blood and righteousness of Christ; then the peace of God, which here is called "great," and elsewhere "that passeth understanding". Some parts of the ocean laugh the sounding-line to scorn. You may let out 1,000, 2,000, even 6,000 fathoms, and still the plumb falls clear. So it is when God's peace, driven from all the world, comes to fold its wings of rest in the heart. It is better than joy, which falters and fluctuates; better than the ecstasy which may have its reactions. Deep, sweet, still, all-pervading—eye hath not seen, nor ear heard, nor heart conceived its like.

And these two rest on each other. The more you know God, the more peace you have; because you find Him more worthy of your trust. We have peace in each other, when we know that each is worthy of all our confidence. Peace grows from less to more; from a condition which is largely experimental to one which is fixed and ever-lasting; and always in proportion to the extended area of our acquaintance with God. Acquaint then thyself with Him, and be at peace; thereby good shall come to thee. Great peace have they that love His law; and nothing shall offend them.

(3) THEIR SAFETY.—The waster fulfils a useful function: the knife that cuts away the dead wood; the fire that eats out the alloy; the winnowing fan that rids the wheat of the chaff; the east wind tearing through the forest; the frost crumbling up the soil; the vast army of animals that devour and destroy. "I have created the waster to destroy." This is the strong Hebrew way of saying that God permits, and overrules, and brings out good by means of the evil that had seemed destructive of all good.

Think it not strange concerning the fiery trial which is to try thee. Be not afraid, when thou seest the smith blowing up the fire in his forge, and bringing forth a weapon, the teeth of which might send a shudder through a stouter heart than thine. Thy God created, and can control him. Nothing which God has made can do more than He permits. Thy Father is over all; and He has said, without hesitation or reserve, that no weapon formed against his own shall prosper, and that they shall condemn all tongues raised against them in judgment.

It is impossible to escape the ordeal. It would not be good for us, if we could. "They shall surely gather against thee." "In the world," said the Master, "ye shall have tribulation. If they have hated and persecuted Me, they will hate and persecute you." But they cannot really hurt. Keep on doing what is right in his sight, with a single eye for his glory, and a simple resolve to do his will. The fire may burn around thee, but only to consume thy bonds; the storm may arise against thee, but the billows which break in thunder on the beach, shall not break one splinter from the cliffs. Do not seek to vindicate or avenge thyself. Be still and know that thy God reigns. He will interpose at the exact hour of need; He will vindicate; He will turn the edge of the weapons of thy foes against themselves, and silence every accusing, whispering, calumniating voice. This is thy heritage; if thou art his servant, thine honour is in the Divine keeping.

This is the City of God, and we walk its streets day by day. We have come to Mount Zion, the city of the living God, the heavenly Jerusalem; its breeze fans our faces, its music fills our ears, its bright and holy inhabitants touch us in the streets, its interests and employments engage our hands. The New Jerusalem, for us at least, has come down from God out of heaven, and is here.

26

OUR GLORIFIED LEADER

*"He is gone—and we remain
In this world of sin and pain;
In the void which He has left,
On this earth of Him bereft.
We have still His work to do;
We can still His path pursue;
Seek Him both in friend and foe,
In ourselves his image show."*

Stanley

(Isaiah 55:4)

There are things which money cannot buy. It were absurd to bring gold or silver, or any such equivalent for them; they are without price. They therefore elude the rich, who have acquired the habit of supposing that money is the only medium of exchange, and who find it hard to think of wealth other than that which passes current in the market; whilst they are within the reach of those who have no money, but who are sorely athirst. What these things are will appear presently. Suffice it only to say that they are contained in a Person, and that it is impossible to have them unless we enter into living union with Him.

It was highly necessary that God should call the attention of the Jewish people to these unpurchasable possessions. Their life in Babylon had become so luxurious. They had so suddenly acquired wealth; they had so easily bartered their spiritual prerogative, as the priests of men, for mercenary consideration, that there was every danger of their losing sight of the great facts of the spiritual world. It was needful, therefore, for them to be reminded that the immortal thirst of the soul cannot be quenched by waters whose source is in the depth of the earth, though the wells be deep as Sychar's; and that its hunger cannot be satisfied with the provision beneath

which the tables of a Dives groan. True satisfaction—
that which is really bread, the fatness that delights the
soul—can only be obtained where the coins of this
world do not pass current ; in fellowship with Him whose
voice is ever speaking in the marts of commerce, saying,
"Ho, every one that thirsteth, come ye! hearken unto
Me! buy wine and milk! eat ye that which is good!"

These gifts of the spiritual world by which the soul
lives are given in covenant ; each man must enter for
himself into covenant-relationship with God. Yet, in the
deepest sense, the covenant has been already made on
the behalf of all faithful souls, by their Representative,
who here looms out amid the mists of the far past in
the unmistakable glory of the Son of Man.

Thus we have three clear issues before us: "The Prince
of Life ; the Everlasting Covenant ; the Abundant Provision which is ours in Him.

(1) THE PRINCE OF LIFE.—"Behold, I have given Him
for a Leader and Commander to the people."

(1) *He was typified in David.* The shepherd boy was
God's gift to Israel, to save his people from the anarchy
into which Saul's wilfulness had plunged them ; to deliver the land from the incursions of the Philistines ;
and to lead them like a flock. God entered into a covenant with him to make him a house, and that his son
should sit upon his throne, assured of the living presence
of Jehovah, and of the certainty of an established throne
for ever. These were the sure mercies of David, when
God appointed him prince over his people (2 Sam. 7:
8-17).

In each of these respects the Almighty entered into
covenant with great David's Greater Son. He has been
constituted Prince. His name is made great. His throne
shall be for ever. His kingdom shall be made sure.
For a great while to come his house shall stand. His
name shall be continued as long as the sun, and men
shall be blessed in Him. All nations shall call Him happy
(Psa. 72). The type was spoilt by David's infidelity and
sin. The pattern of things in the heavens always bear the
soil, the fret, and the tarnish of this world. But even
though this was so, on God's side there was no vacil-
lation, no swerving from his purpose. His mercies were

sure. Much more in the case of Jesus Christ, the eternal purpose cannot miscarry. There can be no failure upon his part to perform the conditions of the covenant; and God will not run back from his word. He hath made with his Son a covenant which is orderly in all things and sure. It were easier to break the procession of day and night, than that one item of its provisions should be invalidated.

(2) *This title is applied to Christ after his resurrection.* Four times only in the New Testament is Christ called Leader or Prince, and always in resurrection. In his sermon in the temple, Peter accuses the Jews of having killed "the Prince of Life," and immediately adds, "whom God raised from the dead" (Acts 3:14, 15). Again, before the Sanhedrin, he affirms that "God exalted Him with his right hand to be a Prince and a Saviour,"—that exaltation evidently referring to the Ascension from the depth of the grave to the right hand of power (Acts 5:31). In the Epistle to the Hebrews we are told that God hath made "the leader of our salvation perfect through sufferings, and hath crowned Him with glory and honour" (Heb. 2:9, 10). And yet again in the same Epistle we are told to look to Jesus, who has sat down at the right hand of the throne of God, as "the Author of faith" (Heb. 12:2). However translated, whether by *Author, Prince, Captain* or *Leader,* it is the same Greek word, and is applied to Christ as risen.

(3) *The original meaning of the word is very interesting.* Etymologically, it means the first of a file of men, and therefore their leader and commanding officer. This conception therefore is presented to our mind, that our Lord is the first of a long procession of souls whom He is leading up from the grave, with its darkness and corruption, through the steeps of air, past principalities and powers, to the very throne of God. He is the First-born from the dead, and therefore Ruler of the kings of the earth. He first, by the resurrection from the dead, has obtained the right to proclaim light to the Gentiles.

If this thought of Christ being the first of a long procession is carried out, in respect to the passages mentioned above, it yields great results. *He leads the dead out of death into life.* There is a close analogy between the life and work of Joshua and of Jesus. After the death of Moses, God gave Joshua to be a witness to the people of truth and righteousness—to be their leader and commander. To make the analogy perfect, we may well suppose that Joshua first passed across the dried bed of the Jordan, hard by the little group of priests standing there, ark on shoulder, and that the long procession of Israel trod in his steps. Whether that were so or not, it is impossible to say. But this, at least, is true, that Christ has preceded us through the waters of Jordan, which always stand for death; and that He will hold them back until every one of the ransomed has passed "clean over Jordan."

He leads the vanquished into the victory of the heavenlies. In his exaltation as Man to the right hand of the throne, He opened a path to be trodden in after ages by a company which no man can number. Where He is, they are to be; as He has overcome, they are to overcome; as He is regnant over principality and power, they are to sit on his throne till their enemies are made the footstool of their feet.

He leads sufferers through suffering to the perfection, which is only possible as the effect of grievous pain, sanctified through the grace of the Holy Ghost. Son though He were, He learned obedience by the things that He suffered; and transformed suffering, showing that it was an alembic, a purifying furnace, a means of discipline, strength, and ennoblement—all of which have become the heritage of the suffering people of God. All who suffer meekly according to the will of God are following in the long procession which He headed.

He leads also the ranks of believers. In the eleventh chapter of the marvellous treatise already quoted we have a roll-call of the heroes of faith; but the writer takes care to tell us that not Abel, though he were the first in time, not Abraham, though first as progenitor, not Moses, though first in the marvels wrought, but Jesus is the true file-leader of faith.

(4) *These conclusions suggested by the New Testament are substantiated and confirmed by the expression used here.* "Thou shalt call a nation that Thou knowest not." To whom can this refer, save to the Gentiles, who were once far off? "Nations that knew not Thee, shall run unto

Thee." Of whom can this be true, save of that vast in-gathering suggested to our Lord by the Greeks who came to Him before He died, and concerning whom He said, "I, if I be lifted up, will draw all men unto Me"? These words are a direct address from the people of God to their directly-given Leader. Thankfully they remind Him that the Holy One of Israel has glorified Him. And when did our Lord receive honour and glory save when, for his obedience unto death, He received a name which is above every name, and in which every knee shall bow, and every tongue confess.

O Glorious Leader of faithful souls! who hast conducted so great an exodus from the grave and the dark domain of selfishness and sin, and from the realm of the transient and material to the unseen and eternal, the sinless and sorrowless world, we, who follow Thee, pray that nations who have not known Thee may run to Thee ; that there may be a great gathering of the peoples around Thy banner ; and that many who are wasting their energy for waters that cannot quench their thirst, and for bread that cannot satisfy their hunger, may follow Thee to the River of the Water of Life, and to the Tree of Life which is in the midst of the Paradise of God!

God has given—wilt thou accept his gift? He gave his only-begotten Son, and with Him will freely give all things. Draw near and take ; and let Him be for thy comfort, sustenance, and salvation, world without end.

(2) THE EVERLASTING COVENANT.—Towards the close of David's life, he sang one brief strain concerning which he was very sure that the Spirit of the Lord was speaking by him, and that his word was upon his tongue. He seems to have had a glimpse of the lost opportunities of his life. He says sadly, that one who rules over men righteously would be like sunrise, as a cloudless dawn, as the tender grass, the joint product of rain and sun. That was what his reign might have been, but the fair ideal had never been realised. He had not always ruled in the fear of God. He had committed iniquity, for which he had been chastened by the rod of men, and with the stripes of the children of men (2 Sam. 7:14, 15 ; 2 Sam. 23:3).

He had been forgiven ; but the natural consequences had remained. His house had not been so with God. Incest, murder, hatred, had rent it ; and his last words make mention of the ungodly who could not be taken unless the hand were armed with sword and spear. Adonijah, Joab, Shimei, and others were as thorns in the side of the aged king. But in spite of all he knew that God's covenant with himself was sure. He had said, "My mercy shall not depart, as I took it from Saul whom I put away before thee." In his own words, the "covenant was ordered in all things and sure."

A similar covenant has been enacted between the Father and the Son as the Representative of the redeemed. God will never be unfaithful to its provisions. The work of the Cross has been definitely accepted on our behalf. The precious Blood has been accounted a sufficient atonement. The obedience and death of Jesus Christ are enough. Those that believe in Him shall never perish. God's mercies to us in Christ are sure. But we must definitely enter into that covenant for ourselves. Note the emphasis. Listen! come! hear! and—I will make an everlasting covenant with *you*.

Men talk much in the present day of the solidarity of the race; and are accustomed to group men in one great family, to the obscuring of the equally true doctrine of individualism. We must not allow these two to collide. Each is necessary to the true development of the soul. It is true that all who repent and believe are included in the provisions of the eternal covenant—entered into in the council-chamber of eternity; but it is equally true there is a personal transaction between God and each soul, by virtue of which it enters into a relationship with God, which neither life nor death, things present nor things to come, can violate or interrupt.

(3) THE ABUNDANT PROVISION.—It is described under several terms—waters, wine, milk, satisfying bread, the good, fatness. We are invited to come for water, and lo! we find a feast prepared at which we sit to eat. All this reminds us of words in the Epistles, the wealth of which surpasses thought. "Blest with all spiritual blessings in the heavenlies in Christ." "All things are yours." "His Divine power hath given to us all things that pertain to life and godliness."

It is too much our habit to pray as though by our entreaty we should obtain for ourselves what we need for life or service. We cry, "Go to! I will pray day and night for this or the other grace; I will buy this power by tears and sighs and many prayers." Oh that we could realise that the table is spread, that there is enough for us, that our name lies between the knife and fork, that the doors stand open, and that we have only to take! Everything that the apostles had is ours. All that God can give is given. All that the soul wants is ready to hand. We have not to ascend into heaven to bring down the grace of God; or to descend into any depth to bring it up. It is nigh, it is here. Eat, O beloved, eat and drink abundantly; there can be no stint for those whom God calls as his guests to sit at the table of his Son. We talk as though the feast were at the end of this dispensation; but the oxen and fatlings are already killed, and all things are now ready. Come ye!

Without money, and without price. And is it really so? Is there indeed nothing to pay? Not after men's usage. We buy by confessions of our need; by bringing our emptiness and want; by being willing to be the pensioners on the bounty of God. To give up yourself, to renounce all faith in prayers and tears and entreaties, to be willing to take as a little child from the open hand of God— this is the purchase money for the priceless wealth of heaven.

Let it never be forgotten that the rich provisions of God's grace can only be enjoyed by those who follow their Leader, Christ, and obey his commands. This Captain of ours demands absolute obedience. If He says, "Come!" we must come, whatever we leave. If He says, "Go!" we must go, into whatever difficulty we plunge, or whatever peril we incur. If He says, "Do this!" there is no appeal. Run to Him, abide in Him, sit with Him in the heavenlies, obey Him! Take Him as God's best gift; give Him the glory of thy homage as the Father has given Him the glory of his own bright home. So shalt thou drink wine and milk, and eat bread that satisfies, and delight thyself in the fatness of his holy temple.

Thus earth may partake somewhat of the blessedness of that eternal world, where it is said that "they follow the Lamb whithersoever He goeth; and they hunger no more, neither thirst any more, neither does the sun strike on them, nor any heat." In fact, the whole Church drinks of the same river, and upon the same conditions. In each world the flock must follow the lead of Christ. In each world they drink of the river of the water of life, proceeding from the throne of God and the Lamb; the one near its source, the other in the lowlands of this world.

27

THE NEAR AND HEAVENLY HORIZONS

"Mine is an unchanging love,
Higher than the heights above,
Deeper than the depths beneath,
Free and faithful, strong as death."

Cowper

(Isaiah 55:9)

The *thoughts of God!* We can form some conception of them through the works of his hand, whether in nature, providence, or redemption. The psalmist describes them as permanent in their endurance; as surpassing the reckoning of human arithmetic; and as being a fathomless deep. It is told of Kepler that, one night, after hours spent in observing the motions of the heavenly bodies, he exclaimed, "I have been thinking over again the earliest thoughts of God." But there are earlier thoughts than those impressed on nature. The love that led to the choice of man in Christ, and will culminate in the glory, is older far. Let us think more often of these thoughts of God, until we cry, "How precious are Thy thoughts unto me, O God! How great is the sum of them!"

The ways of God. He made them known unto Moses; as though He could communicate a more intimate knowledge of his dealings to his favoured servant than was possible to the children of Israel, who were only made cognisant of his acts. God's way is in the sea of mystery; his path lies through the great waters of sorrow. It was the cry of the psalmist that he should be taught his ways; it was the Divine complaint against Israel that they had not known them.

It is of these thoughts and ways that we are told that they are as much above ours as the heavens are above the earth. First, the heavens are so far above the earth, and *therefore so pure*. Second, they are so far, and *therefore so abundant*. Third, they are so far, *and therefore so beneficent*. And in each of these respects they are emblems of the nature and the mercy of God.

(1) SO FAR, AND THEREFORE, SO PURE.—In the firmament of heaven there entereth nothing that worketh abomination or defiles. The miasma with its poison, the smoke belched from the chimney with its dark stain, are powerless to sully the purity of the azure. Meet emblem this of the purity of God, whose name is Holy, and who dwells in the high and holy place. The contrast between heaven and earth in this respect is the contrast between God's thoughts and ways, and man's. Such is evidently the teaching of this passage: "Let the wicked forsake his *way*, and the unrighteous man his *thoughts*. . . . For My *thoughts* are not your thoughts, neither are your ways My *ways*, saith the Lord. For as the heavens," etc.

Of course, man could never emulate the thoughts and ways of God in their measure and movement, their infinitude, or their incomprehensible extent. This is not required; nor is it accounted a sin that we should fall short in the measure and quantity. But since we are made in the image of God, it is evidently possible that we should manifest a strong likeness to his thoughts and ways, so far at least as their *quality* and essential nature are concerned.

The calculations of astronomers prove that there is an identity between the Divine and human mind in arithmetic and mathematics. The transcription of the work of God by the artist or sculptor proves that there is an identity in the appreciation of beauty. The perpetual tendency on the part of man to produce, whether it be a poem or a minster, proves an identity in the creative faculty. Similarly, there must be an identity in the moral and spiritual. What is true to God, is so to us. Love, purity, compassion, humility, are the same in the Divine and in the human. It is by the spectroscope of our own hearts that we are able to determine the elements that compose the being of God. The original creation of man in God's image, and the incarnation, which showed that

180

it was possible for God to think and act through our nature, establish beyond controversy that man can and should think God's thoughts, and tread God's ways. Though his home is on the earth, he is not the child of earth, but of heaven ; and is called to seek, not the things below, but those above, the things of God, and eternity.

The entrance of sin into our world has altered all this. Earth's attraction has proved too strong. The transient and visible, with their appeal to the senses, have ruptured the harmony which the Creator intended to subsist between the Divine and the human, like noble words married to celestial music. It is but too evident. that the imagination of the thoughts of man's heart is only evil continually, and his ways corrupt. By nature, the trend of our thinkings and activities is downward, earthly, sensual, devilish. Hence the awful disparity between the ways and thoughts of God and ours.

It is impossible, therefore, for the natural man to understand God. We can only know one another through the spirit of man which is in us. Our quick human sympathy reveals instantly, and by a flash, what no words could tell. But we must be likeminded before we can read each other. It is equally so as between ourselves and God. The natural man, whose tastes and ways are foreign to God's, can no more receive the things of the Spirit of God, than can a savage understand the thoughts and ways of a highly-cultured, refined, and spiritual man amongst ourselves. "They are foolishness unto him, neither can he know them ; because they are spiritually discerned."

It is impossible, also, for the natural man to please God. God's thoughts are holiness, his ways purity ; but those of the unregenerate are unholy and impure. God's thoughts are love, his ways tenderness ; but those of the unregenerate are self-centred and injurious. God's thoughts are truth, his ways faithful ; whilst those of the unregenerate are insincere and deceptive. How impossible it is, therefore, for those who are in the flesh to please God! They are not subject to the law of God, neither indeed can be.

It is impossible, also, for the natural man to live with God for ever, unless the wicked forsake his ways, and the unrighteous man his thoughts. Whatever the sufferings of the outer darkness may be, those of the inner chamber, to the evil and profane, would be incomparably worse. To the diseased eye, nothing is so excruciatingly painful as the floods of summer sunshine in which age and youth rejoice. And to the unholy soul no suffering would be more awful than to be compelled to live for ever amid the blaze of God's presence, with which it was in perpetual opposition and contrariety. If it were possible for such a one to enter the city of God, with its light above the brightness of the sun, its music, its festal crowds, its holy exercise, the olden cry would be heard exclaiming, "What have I to do with Thee, the Holy One? Thy presence torments me."

It is imperative, then, that the ways and thoughts of the wicked and unrighteous should be forsaken. They must return from Bypath Meadow, and reverse the current of their thinking. The eyes that had been fixed on vanity must be lifted in the track of the ascending Lord; the feet that had almost gone over the precipice to perdition must run in the way of God's commandments; and the will must be so put in the line of God's will, that God may work in it that which is well pleasing in his sight, for the glory of his Holy Name. The Ascension gives us the direction, and the Holy Ghost the power, by which the new and better life shall henceforth be lived (Col. 3: 1–4). Thus the pure life of the heavens may be brought down to our earth, even as it was in the life of our Lord, who during his earthly sojourn did not hesitate to speak of Himself as yet being in heaven (John 3: 13).

(2) SO FAR, AND THEREFORE SO ABUNDANT.—Measure the height of the heavens above the earth; attach yourself to some angel-aeronaut, and let him pilot you through their ample spaces to the confines of our system, where Neptune and Uranus burn with brilliant glory; then across the dark, silent gulf which intervenes between them and the nearest fixed star—a space so great that, supposing our sun were represented by a two-foot globe, it would be equivalent to the distance between our shores and Australia. From that distant point you might pass on to worlds so inconceivably distant, that though their light has been travelling towards us for millenniums, it has never yet reached our world. Thence you might pass to the margin of the ocean of space, where the waves of ether break in music on their shores. Such are the heavens. In truth,

they are higher than the earth; and in precisely the same proportion is the abundance of God's pardon beyond the furthest reach of our imaginings. "He will *abundantly* pardon. *For* my thoughts are not your thoughts; neither are your ways my ways, saith the Lord. For as the heavens are higher," etc.

This is the thought which the apostle expands in one of the most glowing passages on the page of revelation (Rom. 5:12–21). His point is, that whatever was done by sin, and through sin, must be parelleled and out-done by the grace of God. If death came to all men through the trespass of a sinner, of course grace must come to them all through the person and work of the one glorious and unfallen Man, Jesus Christ. If it was pos-sible for death to get such a foothold through one act of selfishness as to reign, it must be equally possible for eternal life to reign through the matchless act of self-denial which shines from the cross. If sin reigned in death, much more must grace reign through righteous-ness unto eternal life. He goes so far as to say that God gave the law that the full virulence and violence of sin might be discovered. It was as though He gave *carte blanche* to sin to do its worst. At the cross, where the dispensation of law culminated, there was an apocalypse, an unveiling, of the exceeding sinfulness of sin. Only God before that had known what sin really was in its essence and possibilities: from that moment the dark secret was revealed to the universe. But if sin, like the dark waters of the Deluge, covered earth's highest mountains, grace in its abundant provisions was as much above it as the heavens were above the floods when they were at their worst.

There is no parallel between our forgiveness and God's. We must not measure his by ours. We say we would forgive if there were more adequate contrition, more complete confession; or we would forgive if the sin were not so wilful and unprovoked; or we will forgive, but we cannot forget. Our forgiveness is not ready, and we are often cautious and chilly towards those who have offended us, but to whom we have become reconciled. With such memories as these, is it wonderful that we can-not realise the completeness of God's forgiveness, nor the full meaning of his assurance that He will remem-ber our sins no more? Leave your miserable standards behind, whether of your own forgiveness, or of those of others; they positively will not help you here; your fathoming lines are utterly useless; your estimates futile. Measure the height of yonder heavens above the earth; and then begin to compute the abundance of God's pardon to those who return to Him, with words of confession on their lips, and true penitence in their hearts.

The prodigal thinks at the very most that he can only expect a stinted pardon, and a servant's fare. That is because his notions of forgiveness range no higher. But the father runs, falls on his neck, kisses him, clothes him with the most sumptuous dress, and seats him at the table with the most royal provision. That is the difference between man's notions of pardon and Christ's.

When God forgives, He ceases to remember; he blots out iniquities as a cloud, and sins as a thick cloud; He does not treat us simply as pardoned criminals, but takes us to his heart as beloved sons; He imputes to us a perfect righteousness; He treats us as though we were credited with the perfect loveliness of the Best-Beloved; He transforms the sad consequences of our sins into blessings, so that as we return from the far country, the mountains break forth into song, the trees of the wood clap their hands; instead of the thorn comes up the fir tree, and instead of the briar the myrtle tree; and these transformations become everlasting memorials of what God's love can do for the repentant sinner. This surely is as much above man's notions of forgiveness as the heavens are high above the earth.

(3) SO FAR, AND THEREFORE SO BENEFICENT.—Because the heavens are so far above the earth, they are able to collect in their ample bosom the moisture of the earth. The clouds, like barges, bear their precious cargo of rain and snow over the parched earth, to drop the one in fertilising streams, and the other as a warm mantle on the upturned furrows. Thus, because the heavens are higher than the earth, the rain cometh down and the snow from heaven, and watereth the earth, and maketh it bring forth and bud, that it may give seed to the sower and bread to the eater.

The very greatness of God is an obligation. Just because He dwells in the ample pavilion of heaven, He is under a moral indebtedness to help us in our low and

fallen state. The possession of power among all right-
minded men constitutes an irresistible argument for the
relief of sorrow and distress; how much more with the
Infinite One, who is Love! If Paul held himself as debtor
to all men, how much more God!

And how graciously and generously He has met the
demand! His word distils as the tender dew, and is pure
and warmth-giving as the snow. Who can tell the number,
pricelessness, or glory of his gifts in Jesus Christ?

> *Streams of mercy, never ceasing,*
> *Call for songs of loudest praise.*

The one question for us all to answer is our response
to these descending influences from the heart of God.
We read, that land which hath drunk the rain that cometh oft upon it, and beareth thorns and thistles, is nigh
unto a curse, and its end is to be burned. Have we thus
recompensed the grace of God, which has fallen on our
souls? Alas for us, if we have! yet even now they may
be changed to myrtles and fir trees. Happy are they who
bring forth herbs meet for Him for whose sake they
have been tilled. Who can this be, save Jesus Christ our
Lord, whose inheritance we are, and who has expended
on us the bloody sweat of his brow, the labour and patience
of long years.

28

THE TRANSFORMATIONS OF GOD'S GRACE

> *"Now—the spirit conflict-riven,*
> *Wounded heart, unequal strife!*
> *Afterward—the triumph given,*
> *And the Victor's crown of Life!*
> *Now—the training, strange and lowly,*
> *Unexplained and tedious now!*
> *Afterward—the Service holy,*
> *And the Master's 'Enter thou!'"*

F. R. Havergal

(Isaiah 55: 12, 13)

The wealth of God's abundant pardon is here set forth
in metaphors which the least imaginative can understand.

Not only were the exiles forgiven, their warfare accomplished, their iniquity pardoned; but they would be restored to the land of their fathers—"Ye shall go out ... ye shall be led forth ..." Not only were they to be restored; but their return was to be one long triumphal march. Nature herself would celebrate it with joyful demonstration; mountains and hills would break forth into singing, and all the trees of the field would clap their hands.

But even this was not all. One of the necessary results of the depopulation of the land of Israel was the deterioration of the soil. Vast tracts had passed out of cultivation; the terraces, reared on the slopes of the hills with so much care, had become heaps of stones; where corn had waved in the rustling breeze, or luscious fruits had ripened in the autumn sunshine, there was the sad fulfilment of the prediction, "They shall smite upon their breasts for the pleasant fields, for the fruitful vine. Upon the land of My people shall come up thorns and briers" (Isa. 32:12, 13). But this, too, was to be reversed. Literally and metaphorically, there was to be a complete reversal of the results of former sins and backslidings. Instead of the thorn would come up the fir tree, and instead of the briar would come up the myrtle tree; and it would be to the Lord for a name, for an everlasting sign, that would not be cut off. An everlasting sign! That surely indicates that sacred lessons are hidden under this prediction, which are of permanent interest and importance. Let us seek them in the light of other scriptures.

"Unto Adam He said, cursed is the ground for thy sake; in sorrow shalt thou eat of it all the days of thy life; thorns also, and thistles shall it bring forth unto thee."

"And the soldiers plaited a crown of thorns, and put it on His head."

"There was given me a thorn in the flesh ... Concerning this thing I besought the Lord thrice, that it might depart from me. And He said unto me, My grace is sufficient for thee."

Our thought naturally divides itself thus: The Thorns and Briars of Life; The Royalty of Suffering them; The Transformations of Grace.

186

(1) THE THORNS AND BRIARS OF LIFE.—In many cases we reap what others have sown; in some we sow for ourselves; in others we suffer from our neglect. We have failed to use our opportunities; and therefore crops of rank growth cover the acres of the past, and thistledown hovers in clouds, threatening the future.

Ill-health is surely one. Many of us, through God's goodness, have known but few days of sickness in our lives; others have known as few of complete health. Disease fastened on them in early life has sapped their strength, is slowly working its way to the citadel of life. For some, the excesses of their ancestors—for others, their own—have sown the furrow with the seeds of bitter harvests, which they have no alternative than to reap. Dyspepsia, cancer, the slow progress of paralysis along the spinal cord, nervous weakness and depression—these are some of the many ills to which our flesh is heir; and they are thorns indeed. Paul's thorn was probably ophthalmia.

Bad children are another. Did David not mean this when he said that his house was not so with God; and that the ungodly, like thorns, must be thrust away with the armed hand?
Was he not thinking of Absalom and Adonijah, and others in his home circle? He was certainly describing the experience of many a parent whose life has been embittered by stubborn, dissolute, and extravagant children. When the daughters make unfortunate marriages, and sons spread their sails to every gale of passion, there are thorns and briars enough to make misery in the best appointed and most richly-furnished homes.

Strong predispostions and tendencies towards evil may be classed among the thorns. To be of a jealous or envious temperament; to have an inordinate love for praise and flattery; to be cursed with the clinging habit of impurity, intemperance, or greediness; to be of an irascible or phlegmatic disposition; and to be so liable to doubts that all the affirmations of fellow-disciples fall on dull and irresponsive ears—this is to be beset with thorns and briars, as though all the goodness of a field should go to waste in weeds.

Compulsory association with uncongenial companions

187

in the workshop or the home. When day and night we are obliged to bear the galling yoke of fellowship with those who have no love for God, no care for man. When the enemy daily taunts, the sword penetrates to the bone, and the reproach eats like acid into the flesh; when we pick our way along paths thick-set with traps, we know something of these cruel thorns. The old punishment of the men of Succoth at the hands of Gideon has its counterpart still: "And he took the elders of the city, and thorns of the wilderness, and briars, and with them he thrashed the men of Succoth."

Difficulties that bar our progress, like hedges of prickly thorns in some tangled forest, may be included in this enumeration. Competition in commercial life makes thorny the path of many a man of business. Perplexities and worries, annoyances, and vexations, fret us almost beyond endurance; the tender flesh is pitilessly torn, the heart bleeds secretly, hope dies in the soul; we question the wisdom and goodness of God in having made or permitted such a world where such things were possible.

Each life has experiences like these. Messengers of Satan come to buffet us all, making us ask the Lord— not once, nor twice, but often—if the stake may not be taken out of the flesh, and the soul set free to serve Him. Surely, we argue, we could live nobler and more useful lives, if only we were free. "Not so," says the Lord. "I cannot take away the thorn—it is the only means of royalty for thee; but I will give thee my all-sufficient grace."

(2) ROYALTY THROUGH THORNS.—It is very remarkable that the sign of the curse became, on the brow of Christ, the insignia of Royalty. The lesson is obvious—that He has transformed the curse into a blessing; that He has discovered the secret of compelling it to yield royalty.

There was some dim hint of this in the words of the primæval curse on the ground, "Cursed is the ground *for thy sake ;* thorns also and thistles it shall bring forth unto thee." What can this mean, except that there was an ulterior design in this infliction on the material world? It is not very clear what is implied in this sentence on the ground. Almost certainly there were thorns and thistles before Adam's sin brought a blight on God's fair world; but probably from that moment they became more prolific or the conditions that had been unfavourable to their growth became more favourable, or malign hands were permitted to scatter their seeds afar. But, however it befell, there can be no doubt that God's purpose was wholly benevolent. Cursed is the ground *for thy sake;* that is, out of the obduracy of the soil and its tendency to breed thorns and thistles, will come to thee the best and highest blessing.

Surely this has been verified. Where has man attained his noblest development? in lands where kindly nature has been most prodigal of her good gifts; where the soil has only needed scratching to yield a bountiful return? where life has been free from care, as that of bees among the limes? No, not there. By her, the bountiful provision of all they needed for their sustenance and comfort, Nature has enervated her children, men have become inert and sensual, ease-loving and muscleless. But where the soil has been unkindly, the climate inhospitable, the struggle for existence hard, the presence of the thorn ever menacing the cultivated patch, and threatening to invade garden or field; where every endeavour has been required to wring subsistence from the unwilling ground—there man has arisen to his full height, and put forth all his glorious strength of brain and sinew. It is through nature's churlishness and niggardliness, through man's long wrestle with her in the dark, through the bearing of travail and sorrow of toil, that the supple crafty, characterless Jacobs have come forth as Israels, crowned princes with God.

Probably this is what is meant in the thorn-crown on the brow of Christ. It teaches that man can only attain his true royalty by meeting, enduring, and overcoming these elements in life, which forbode only disaster and loss. The purpose of God is wholly benevolent in the stern discipline to which He is subjecting thee. He has set thee down among those thorns to give thee an opportunity of changing the wilderness into a paradise; and in the act of transformation thou wilt suddenly find thyself ennobled and transfigured. Around thy brow the thorns—borne, mastered, subdued—shall weave themselves into a crown, and thou shalt glory in thy infirmities.

What a magnificent conception this gives of the possibilities of sorrow! Too many estimable people fret against God's ordering of their lives, and his permission of the evils which afflict them. Like Paul, they are always praying to be delivered. But God is too good to answer these blind requests. The thorns remain; they must grapple with them, as did the old monks, when they chose some tangled swamp as the site of a new monastery. No alternative is afforded. And in proportion as we patiently submit ourselves to our Father's appointment, we come to see the reasonableness and beneficence of his design, and find ourselves adopting the thistle as our badge; we discover that it has been the means of unfolding and perfecting our character, of giving royalty and dignity to our demeanour, and making us kings by right of conquest, as well as by right of birth.

(3) THE TRANSFORMATIONS OF GRACE.—"Instead of the thorn shall come up the fir tree; and instead of the briar the myrtle tree." "My grace is sufficient for thee; my strength is made perfect in weakness." "I will therefore glory in my infirmities."

(1) God gives us new views of dark things. What we thought was punishment, turns out to be the chastening of a Father's love. The knife is not of the destroyer, but of the surgeon. What seemed to be unto death, is shown to be achieving a fuller life. The fire that had threatened to consume, only shrivels our bonds so that we walk freely over the glowing embers. We are permitted to stand beside God on the Mount, while He passes by and proclaims his name, and gives his reasons, and takes us behind his providences. That illness was sent to rid the system of a poison-taint that had else proved fatal. That child was permitted to be deformed by a terrible accident, because in no other way could she have been saved from a dark temptation, to which she must have yielded. That commercial disaster befell, because the young children of the household would have been enervated by too much luxury. The thorns change to myrtles when God shows his reasons.

(2) God makes our sorrow and losses occasions for giving more grace. There are two ways of helping the soul bent double under some crushing burden. It may be removed; or additional strength, equal to its weight,

may be inbreathed. The latter is God's choice way of dealing with his children. And if we were wise, we should not pray for the extraction of the thorn; but claim the greater grace. Oh, how precious the trial is then! How many a sufferer has had to bless God for pain! To how many the rack has seemed like a bed of down, and the torture-chamber the vestibule of heaven! Thorns, under such emotions, are changed to fir trees, and briars to myrtles.

(3) The grace of God actually transforms awkward and evil dispositions, both in ourselves and others. Softness becomes meekness; cowardice gentleness; impulsiveness enthusiasm; meanness thrift; niggardliness generosity; cruelty consideration for others; irritability and vehemence patience and long suffering. God did not destroy the Roman Catholic pulpits at the Reformation—he did better, He filled them with Gospel-preachers. Similarly, He does not destroy any of our natural characteristics, when He brings us to Himself; He only eliminates the evil and develops the good. The evil tenant goes forth, making room for the new and holy spirit. Where sin had reigned unto death, grace now reigns unto eternal life. The thorns of passion and temper are replaced by fir trees, and the briars by myrtles. He takes the heart of stone out of our flesh, and gives us a heart of flesh. "In the habitation of jackals, where they lay, is grass with reeds and rushes."

(4) How glad is the wife, when, instead of the brute-like cruelty which reigned in her husband's life, there is gentleness and consideration. How rejoiced is the mother Monica, when her Augustine is no longer the slave of passion; but clothed, subdued, restored to his right mind, and seated at the feet of Jesus! How significant of the power of Christ, to see a nation of savages so transformed that the arts of civilization and the practices of Christianity flourish, where once the cannibal dance and demon worship held undisputed possession.

(5) When the discipline has done its work, it is removed. The Great Husbandman knows well the delicacy of the grain, and He will not always be threshing. Thou hast had thy full experience of thorns and briars, and hast borne and not fainted; but now, since the lesson has been learnt with lowly submission, the discipline will be removed. Thy Joseph lives, and thou shalt see him again

and clasp him to thine arms. Thou shalt embrace a Samuel, whose prattle will make thee forget the smarts of the adversary. Thou shalt receive seven times as much as was swept away from thee so suddenly. Thou shalt come again out of the land of the enemy. Instead of the thorn, the fir; instead of the briar, the myrtle: because they have accomplished the purpose for which they were sent.

These glowing predictions were partially fulfilled in the restoration of Israel under Ezra and Nehemiah; and no doubt they would have been more fully realised if there had been more perfect faith in the Divine promises.

These glowing words, however, shall be perfectly fulfilled in those coming days when Israel shall turn to the land from all lands whither her people have been scattered. Their conversion, the apostle tells us, shall inaugurate the times of refreshing, of which the prophets have spoken from the beginning of the world. Then will creation be delivered from the bondage of corruption into the glorious liberty of the children of God. Then shall the mountains be orchestras of songs, and the trees vocal with melody. Then shall the ancient curse be removed from off the earth, and the malignant influence of the great enemy of God's work be for ever at an end. Then shall earth smile and sing, as in the day of her creation. It shall be to the Lord for a name, for an everlasting sign that shall not be cut off. And the story shall be recited through the universe, for evermore, of the sufficiency of God's love to cope with and overcome every manifestation of evil and self-will that may rear itself against its sway.